THE L♥VE

EIGHT LITTLE THINGS THAT MAKE A BIG DIFFERENCE IN YOUR MARRIAGE

LIST

Resources by Les and Leslie Parrott

Books
Becoming Soul Mates
Getting Ready for the Wedding
Love Is
The Marriage Mentor Manual
Meditations on Proverbs for Couples
Questions Couples Ask
Relationships
Relationships Workbook
Saving Your Marriage Before It Starts
Saving Your Marriage Before It Starts Workbook for Men
Saving Your Marriage Before It Starts Workbook for Women
Saving Your Second Marriage Before It Starts
Saving Your Second Marriage Before It Starts Workbook for Men
Saving Your Second Marriage Before It Starts Workbook for Women
When Bad Things Happen to Good Marriages
When Bad Things Happen to Good Marriages Workbook for Men
When Bad Things Happen to Good Marriages Workbook for Women

Video Curriculum—ZondervanGroupware™
Relationships
Saving Your Marriage Before It Starts
Mentoring Engaged and Newlywed Couples

Audio Pages®
Relationships
Saving Your Marriage Before It Starts
Saving Your Second Marriage Before It Starts
When Bad Things Happen to Good Marriages

Books by Les Parrott III
Control Freak
Helping Your Struggling Teenager
High Maintenance Relationships
The Life You Want Your Kids to Live
Seven Secrets of a Healthy Dating Relationship
Once Upon a Family

Books by Leslie Parrott
If You Ever Needed Friends, It's Now
God Loves You Nose to Toes (children's book)

DRS. LES AND LESLIE PARROTT

THE

LVE

EIGHT LITTLE THINGS THAT MAKE A BIG DIFFERENCE IN YOUR MARRIAGE

LIST

ZONDERVAN™

GRAND RAPIDS, MICHIGAN 49530 USA

We want to hear from you. Please send your comments about this book to us in care of the address below. Thank you.

GRAND RAPIDS, MICHIGAN 49530 USA

WWW.ZONDERVAN.COM

ZONDERVAN™

The Love List
Copyright © 2002 by Les and Leslie Parrott

Requests for information should be addressed to:
Zondervan, *Grand Rapids, Michigan 49530*

Library of Congress Cataloging-in-Publication Data

Parrott, Les.
    The love list : eight little things that make a big difference in your marriage /
by Les and Leslie Parrott.
        p. cm.
    Includes bibliographical references.
    ISBN 0-310-24850-7
    1. Marriage.   2. Parrott, Leslie L., 1964-   II. Title.
HQ734 .P213 2002
306.81—dc21
{C}   2002005295

Interior design by Tracey Moran

Printed in the United States of America

---

02 03 04 05 06 07 08 /❖ DC/ 10 9 8 7 6 5 4 3 2 1

To Jerry and Sharyn Regier
A couple whose vision
has done more for building better marriages
than most people will ever know

CONTENTS

ACKNOWLEDGMENTS

This small book required a big vision from the Focus on the Family publishing team. Kurt Bruner, Al Janssen, Ray Seldomridge, and everyone else who sat around a conference table with us in Colorado Springs helped plant the seeds for the book you hold in your hands. Thanks for your desire to partner with us on this and other projects. As always, our Zondervan family—Bruce Ryskamp, Scott Bolinder, Sandy Vander Zicht, Lori VandenBosch, Angela Scheff, John Topliff, Greg Steilstra, Joyce Ondersma, and Jackie Aldridge—worked in their usual gracious style to make this joint project happen. It is nearly impossible to exaggerate how much you mean to us. Mindy Galbreath, our personal assistant, makes our lives easier in countless ways and always amazes us with her unwavering enthusiasm to help us fulfill our mission and vision. Janice Lundquist, our publicist extraordinaire, works her magic for us in so many ways that we cannot imagine life without her. George Toles, our late-night-email pal, lent his professional creativity to this work and we are grateful. And finally, we want to acknowledge the countless couples who have attended our seminars, attended our classes, been in our counseling offices, and read our previous books. Your comments and questions are the inspiration for this one. We hope and pray the eight little habits you read about in the following pages will serve as another effective tool for helping you build the marriage of your dreams.

LES AND LESLIE PARROTT
SEATTLE, WASHINGTON

Introduction:

THE SECRET OF "THE LIST"

> We must not, in trying to think about how we can make a big difference, ignore the small daily differences we can make which, over time, add up to big differences that we often cannot foresee.
>
> MARIAN WRIGHT EDELMAN

On any given night at our house, about the time our local nightly news airs, you're likely to find both of us perusing the cereal boxes lined up in our kitchen pantry for a late-night snack. Bran Flakes or Frosted Flakes? Shredded Wheat or Special K? It's a scene that has occurred countless times over the course of nearly two decades of marriage. We never planned this nightly ritual; it just happened. And now it's reflexive. A habit. Whoever gets there first typically sets out a bowl and spoon for the other. We do it by instinct, and this seemingly inconsequential and mundane act at the end of our day has become one of the many panels in the quilt of behaviors we've sewn together as a couple.

Every husband and wife, knowingly or not, has dozens of deeds similar to this that they do out of habit—some more helpful to the relationship than others. But rarely are these little habits intentional. They simply evolve. For example, a couple might make the bed together most days. They might read the paper on the front stoop most Saturday mornings. They may visit a favorite park most months, or maybe they always have Chinese food on New Year's Eve. All good things. So what's our point? Every day, every week, every month, and every year, we cut long-lasting grooves or habits into our relationship. We do so without thinking. Yet in the daily grind, few couples realize that, with a little thought and a little intention, they could consciously cultivate a set of specific habits known to work wonders.

After years of studying couples who live and love to the fullest, couples in the top ten percent, we now know what behaviors are bound to increase marital satisfaction for the rest of us. We now know that an intentional couple can revolutionize their relationship—whether it be floundering on the rocks or sailing along at a good clip. Couples everywhere who want to step out of the quiet routine of mediocrity and live life to the fullest, couples who want to love each other to the fullest can do so—if they know the secret of "The Love List."

Cutting a New Groove in Your Relationship

I (Les) have always liked lists. Shopping lists. Honor lists. Wish lists. Lists of goals and dreams. My favorite is the common to-do list. I live by it. Maybe you do too. And if so, you know the wonderful feeling of checking an item off your list. With a simple check mark we know we've accomplished something we set out to do. We've made progress. That little check tells us we've taken another step—big or small—in the direction we want to go.

Short and to the point. That's the value of a good list. And we intend to make that the primary value of this book too. We cut straight to what you can do—starting today— to make your marriage better. How do we do this? By giving you the ultimate to-do list for couples. It's a proven list for pin-pointing specific behaviors, actions, and habits sure to keep your love life running at its peak.

But here's what most people don't know about a to-do list: Simply having it in your possession dramatically increases your chances of reaching your goals. Research has shown that people who make a tangible list and keep it handy are far more likely to achieve their goals than others who have the very same desires but don't make a list.

So we ask you, what's on your list? Do you have one? Do you have a tangible to-do list for making your marriage—one of the most important relationships on earth—all it was meant to be? We hope so, but if you are like the majority of couples, you probably don't. Sure, you've thought about things you'd like to incorporate into your relationship, but like a flare that quickly fades, the ideas pass through your mind for a moment only to be blown away by the next breeze of routine life.

That's why we wrote this book. We've seen far too many well-intentioned couples yearning to enjoy their love life to the fullest but never considering a strategic plan for doing so. They are simply lulled into a mediocre marriage that never reaches its potential. The to-do list provided in this book can change that.

The Love List—or the eight healthy habits, as we call them—is within reach of every couple. Let us allay some potential fears right at the start. The items on this list are not extravagant. They won't cost you more money. They aren't going to require inordinate amounts of time. And they are not just for the romantically gifted. The Love List, short and to the point, is not for perfect people. It's for busy couples who sometimes bicker, get stressed out, have communication meltdowns, struggle with money, are not always sure how to discipline their kids, and all the rest. In other words, the Love List is for real life. Plus, it's fun. It focuses on things you can do, and when you follow it, you will see results almost immediately.

How the Love List Works

The Love List begins by enumerating two things you can do once *each day*. For example, it will ask you to find something that makes you both laugh. Do this every day. You already know that laughter joins your spirits, but you've probably never intentionally set out to find something funny together. We'll show you how.

The Love List will reveal two things to do *each week* in your marriage. It will ask you to boost your partner's self-esteem, for example. Not a tall order for some, but you'd be surprised how many couples overlook the value of this simple ritual—or at least don't understand what they are missing when they neglect it. We'll show you how to buoy up your partner with encouragement.

Next, the Love List will point you to two things to do *each month*. Ridding yourselves of harmful residue is an example from this part of the list. Every marriage, no matter how good, is bound to acquire a buildup of unhealthy attitudes and behaviors. Gunk is inevitable when you live day in and day out with someone. And, yet again, most couples rarely take the time for cleaning the system, for keeping the engine of their marriage tuned up. The chapter on this item of the list will give you several strategies for doing just that.

The final portion of the Love List points you to two important exercises you will conduct on a *yearly* basis. One of them is to chart your course for the coming year. We'll show you why this makes such a significant difference for couples, when it is most optimal to do so, and how to do it.

All in all, the Love List will give you eight healthy habits to cultivate. In our work with newlyweds, we tell them to choose their ruts carefully because they are going to be in them for a long time. And they are. We are creatures of habit; there's no denying it. Yet those habits can be honed to be more healthy, more positive, and more productive. We can step out of our mundane ruts and cut new grooves in our marriage that will serve us well—if we live by the Love List.

Before you start, we have two words of caution, each reflecting our own personal disposition toward lists.

The Danger of Living with Lists—Les's Perspective

Architect Frank Lloyd Wright once told of an incident that seemed insignificant at the time, but had a profound influence on the rest of his life. The winter he was nine, he went walking across a snow-covered field with his no-nonsense uncle. As the two of them reached the far end of the field, his uncle stopped him. He pointed out his own tracks in the snow, straight and true as an arrow's flight, and then young Frank's tracks meandering all over the field. "Notice how your tracks wander aimlessly from the fence to the cattle to the woods and back again," his uncle said. "And see how my tracks aim directly to my goal. There is an important lesson in that."

Years later the world-famous architect liked to tell how this experience had greatly contributed to his philosophy in life. "I determined right then," he'd say with a twinkle in his eye, "not to miss most things in life, as my uncle had."

It's a good lesson, one I've tried to learn myself. Maybe like you, I can become so compelled by my to-do list (it's neatly organized on my electronic date book) that I miss out on the spontaneity of a moment that offers far more than the satisfaction of completing another task. And maybe like you, I can become so driven to check tasks and goals off my list, I never stop to smell the proverbial roses, thinking I'll do that when I'm finished with my list. Like countless others, if I'm not careful, I run the risk of spending my entire life preparing to live.

Are you in the same category? Are you task oriented? Do you stay straight on course, rarely veering for fun? This discipline certainly has its place, but not around the Love List. As you begin this journey with your partner, lighten up. The behaviors and activities on the list are not meant to become ritualistic compulsions. They are not an end in themselves. They are a means to a deeper, more fulfilling love life with your spouse. So take a deep breath, relax, and enjoy the journey as you check things off the Love List in due course.

The Danger of Living Without Lists—Leslie's Perspective

Now, those of us who are happy to meander through life without an intentional plan face another kind of hazard. We may be missing out on more than we know, and it's time we wake up and smell the check boxes. It's time we recognize the advantages of having a few "to-dos"—especially for our marriage. Sure, we're content to go with the flow, dabble in this and dabble in that. Our free-spirited ways bring joy and spontaneity to life for the very reason that we are not slaves to a perpetual list of tiring tasks.

But the Love List is not your typical to-do list. Speaking from personal experience, I've come to view the eight healthy habits of loving couples more like a work of art Les and I are continually creating. It's not monotonous. It's not mundane. Every item on this list breathes freshness into our relationship—just when we need it most.

I've also come to liken the Love List to a compass. It keeps us headed in the right direction. It keeps us going where we both want to go. So, know this: I'm not particularly fond of to-do lists. I'm spontaneous to the core. Maybe you are too. Maybe you are a free spirit. If so, you are also a kindred spirit for me. I understand. You probably feel uneasy about the idea of attaching a to-do list to your love life. But don't throw the idea out until you've given it a chance.

Here's why. Truth be told, I can go for months and never make a list. I'm content to do whatever I think of doing from moment to moment. But once Les and I started putting the Love List into practice in our own marriage, the results amazed me. We are more in tune, more fulfilled, and more in love whenever we live by the Love List.

The Promise of the Love List

A few small actions—practiced on a daily, a weekly, monthly, and yearly basis—can change everything for a couple. Little, deliberate behaviors quietly lavish love on a marriage. There's no need for most of us to get bogged down in an intricate and elaborate overhaul of our relationship. The majority of couples can maximize their love life by internalizing a simple list of loving behaviors and activities that will soon become habits. And in return, these healthy habits will erect an impenetrable fortress, known as a great marriage.

But remember this: A great marriage is not built quickly. It is constructed thought by thought, action by action. It happens year upon year. We are always in process. Always growing. But as we live the Love List in our marriage, we can place our heads on our pillows each night knowing we have done our best. And that's a gift. Victor Hugo said it this way: "When you have laboriously accomplished your daily task, go to sleep in peace. God is awake." So true. And God will do his work in us and in our marriage.

Once a Day . . .

Marriage is like vitamins: we supplement each other's minimum daily requirements.

KATHY MOHNKE

Once a Day . . .

TAKE TIME TO TOUCH
(IF ONLY FOR A MINUTE)

> *Skin cells offer a direct path into the deep reservoir of emotion we metaphorically call the human heart.*
>
> PAUL BRAND

Four years ago we gave birth to our first child, a little boy. And when we say "little," we mean it. After a difficult pregnancy that included two months of bed rest at home and several weeks in the hospital for Leslie, John came into the world—early. Three months early, to be exact. He weighed just over a pound. He was so tiny Les's wedding band easily slipped over John's entire hand, up and over his elbow, and clear to his shoulder, where it still had lots of wiggle room.

John was rushed immediately to the neonatal intensive care unit where he was hooked up to more medical machinery than we knew existed. Doctors thought he might be blind and have numerous developmental problems. He was there for three weeks before they finally released him, tethered to an oxygen tank—the smallest baby ever to be released from Swedish Hospital in Seattle.

Today, John is four years old, and aside from a large surgery scar on his tummy, you would never know he had such a challenging start. We think of him as our miracle baby. Many in his condition don't survive, and precious few who do have as few health concerns as John. We don't know how else to explain it but to say that God worked a miracle in his tiny body.

Of course we did our part too. John rested in a plastic isolet, designed with small portals where we were eventually allowed to reach in and touch him. On occasion the nurses let us change his tiny diapers (known on the preemie ward as "wee-pees"). And as John grew accustomed to our touches, we learned more about the importance of touching him. With a university library at our disposal, we researched how we could help our son make progress. And our studies brought us to a conviction we hold even more firmly today: There is power in human touch.

Study after study revealed how valuable touch could be for our struggling son. At the University of Miami, for example, researchers found that premature babies who were massaged had a forty-seven percent increase in weight gain and went home an average of six days earlier than infants who were not massaged. At eight months of age, these babies were also better able to calm themselves and continued to show better weight gain and intellectual and motor development compared to babies who hadn't received the massages.

Today John is one of the happiest and most loving little guys. And one of the lasting lessons we learned from his ordeal is the immeasurable value of human touch. Not just for premature babies, but for all of us—and especially for our soul mate.

What a Tender Touch Will Do for Your Marriage

Press the rewind button on your marriage for a moment. Backtrack to some of the most romantic and meaningful moments the two of you have ever shared. Can you picture two or three? Chances are that those most memorable moments are etched into your memory bank because they involved a tender touch from the one you love—the holding of your hand, a gentle caress on your cheek, or an arm around your shoulder. And that touch sealed the moment in your memory, never to be forgotten. Touch does that for couples. It is a way of writing in our collective diary to recall the moments we treasure. Anthropologist Helen Fisher, in her book *Anatomy of Love*, describes the importance of touch this way: "Human skin is like a field of grass, each blade a nerve ending so sensitive that the slightest graze can etch into the human brain a memory of the moment."

Without a doubt, physical touch is critical to building romance and intimacy in your marriage. And we don't mean touch only as it relates to sexual play. We are talking about a tender touch while your partner is doing almost any ordinary task. A gentle squeeze on your partner's shoulder as she is preparing a meal, or a soft rub on his back as he is reading a book can communicate loving messages in ways our words never can. There is simply no way to say more persuasively "You are not alone," "I appreciate you," "I'm sorry," or "I love you" than through touch.

Touching your spouse is a language that often speaks more eloquently than words. Sheldon Van Auken, writing about his marriage to Davy in the book *A Severe Mercy*, illustrates the profoundness of touch: "Davy had crept near to me still crouching and I put my arm about her, and she snuggled close. Neither of us spoke, not so much as a whispered word. We were together, we were close, we were overwhelmed by a great beauty. I know that it seemed to us both that we were completely one: we had no need to speak."

For this reason, we dedicate this chapter to helping you make a tender touch a daily habit—if only for a minute.

Ensuring a Tender Touch Each Day of Your Marriage

No one can dispute the value of tender touch between husband and wife. The trick is cultivating this valuable practice on a daily basis. In an effort to bring this important habit into our marriage, we asked dozens of couples how they do just that. Here are a few of their suggestions.

Talk about touch.

Because physical touch is so important to building an intimate marriage, we urge you to talk about it with each other and evaluate your attitude toward it. Why? Because everyone has a unique touch factor. Explore how touch was used in the home you grew up in. Did your mom and dad touch much? Has their model of touching shaped you for better or worse and in what ways? Assuming, like most couples, that you don't always have the same level of need for touch, do the homes you grew up in help to explain why this is so? Or do you think it is more a gender issue?

Talk to each other about how you like to be touched and how you don't like to be touched. Be specific. Maybe paying the bills makes you uptight, and you want to have your space during that time. Claim your "no-touch zones." Knowing when not to touch a spouse is just as important as knowing

Assessing Your Personal Touch Factor

So how's your touch life? Are you getting and giving your daily dose of human touch to each other? The following self-test will help you measure how much touch your marriage enjoys. So take a moment, individually, to answer these questions as honestly as you can, then compare your answers with each other.

T F I know exactly when my partner most appreciates a tender touch.

T F We enjoy a genuine and lasting embrace every day.

T F I'd say we touch each other more than most couples do.

T F I can remember exactly when and where we enjoyed a hug yesterday.

T F We almost always steal at least a quick kiss when reconnecting.

T F When we gently touch and caress each other, it isn't just a signal for sex.

T F If asked to describe exactly how my partner likes to be touched, I'd have no problem describing it.

T F We give each other massages every couple weeks or so.

T F I have used touch on occasion to defuse a tense moment between us.

T F I can recall a specific time when a touch between us conveyed more than words ever could.

Add up the number of "true" responses. If it is eight or higher, you are well on your way to enjoying a daily dose of tender touch. If your score isn't that high, you will certainly benefit from the tips we offer in this chapter for finding creative ways to bring touch into each and every day of your marriage.

when to touch. Let your partner know when you really appreciate a good shoulder massage. Maybe it's while you are reading the paper or while you are standing at the kitchen sink. Or maybe because paying the bills makes you uptight, it is an especially good time for a nice caress. You get the point. Make your wishes known. Take the guesswork out of physical touch by communicating.

Have you had a hug today?

Several years ago as graduate students living in Pasadena, California, we attended a lecture on Valentine's Day by the acclaimed Leo Buscaglia. A professor at University of Southern California, Dr. Buscaglia was wildly popular at the time with several best-selling books, a PBS series, and a national speaking schedule. We enjoyed his inspiring and lively lecture, but what amazed us the most was the huge line of people that formed at the conclusion of his talk. It wound around the entire auditorium. "What are they lining up for?" we asked a fellow attendee. He looked startled that we didn't know and simply said, "A hug." And he was right. Several hundred people queued up for a quick hug from the "the hug doctor." We haven't seen anything like it before or since. And it certainly made an impression.

Some weeks later, by coincidence, I (Les) happened to cross paths with Dr. Buscaglia in a gourmet grocery store. I couldn't help but ask him, "Why do all those people line up to be hugged by you?"

He laughed, but replied seriously, "A hug helps people make it through tough times and lifts the spirit of anyone who is already flying high." It was a question he'd obviously been asked before. As I was about to say thanks, he leaned toward me and gave me a hug—right there in the frozen food section!

Truth is, I'm not the huggy type. And I didn't really need a hug from the famous doctor, but I'll take a hug from my wife any day.

Would you believe there is a World Hug Week? It's true. The sponsoring group believes the world would be a better place if there were a massive movement to embrace our loved ones for five seconds at some point during this week. Silly as it sounds, they're probably right. A five-second hug goes a long way—especially when it comes to getting your daily requirement of touch in marriage. Have you made hugging a habit? If not, we offer a simple suggestion: Ask for one. "May I have a hug?" is all it takes. Say thanks, hello, or good-bye with a hug. Soon you'll have the hug habit.

Get a massage without the high-priced spa.

A few months ago we were guests at a banquet in a ballroom at an Atlanta hotel. In the standard mingling that follows such an occasion, a friend introduced us to a woman who writes for the legendary comedian Bob Hope. Well into his nineties, Mr. Hope doesn't call on his writers like he used to, but she still has contact with him and obviously shares his renowned sense of humor. "So tell me something about Bob Hope I don't know," Les asked her. She thought for a second, then replied, "He gets a massage every day."

Wow! How interesting. The conversation immediately turned to how luxurious it would be to have a personal masseuse that works magic on sore muscles every day. Of course most of us don't have the financial resources of a celebrity like Bob Hope to hire such a person, but if you're married, you do have a spouse that can serve as a pretty good stand-in on occasion.

We have some friends that celebrated their tenth wedding anniversary at a resort in Maui. One of their highlights was a "couple's massage" where a professional trained them to massage each other so that they could enjoy this gift even when they weren't at the spa. Not a bad idea. Bottom line, as a husband and wife, you don't have to employ a personal masseuse or pay a high-priced spa to enjoy the benefits that come from a massage.

Remember the two most important minutes of your marriage.

Let me (Les) speak to the husband for a moment. How do you greet your wife at the end of the day when you have pulled into the driveway and walked through your front door? Are you like me? "I'm home!" I shout out—as if the house is to come to attention and someone is supposed to play "Hail to the Chief." Next, I usually ask, "What's for dinner?" Then, "Did you get the mail?" And the final question in my ceremonial homecoming is "Any calls?"

Maybe you don't do that at all. Good for you. But if you are like me, then you are also like the majority of men who enter their domicile at the end of a work day and head straight for the most comfortable chair to unwind. At least you're like I used to be. A couple years ago I had an awakening when I read some research on the two most important minutes of your marriage. What are they? You got it—the first two minutes when you walk in the door after a day at work.

Experts agree that how you greet each other at the end of your day, after walking through the front door, sets the tone for your entire evening together. What's more, if you greet each other with a tender touch, you immediately release biochemicals in you and your partner that make both of you feel better. Sounds too good to be true, but it's not.

So the next time you announce your return to your castle, whether you are the husband or the wife, do it with a gentle touch, and you'll reap the reward almost instantly.

Catch a kiss—even on the run.

Some years ago we wrote a little book that plucked thirty-one relevant verses for couples from the book of Proverbs. For each verse we wrote an accompanying meditation and prayer, and we titled the book *Like a Kiss on the Lips.* Why that title? Because, as Proverbs says, "An honest answer is like a kiss on the lips." And with that book's publication we have had dozens of couples write us about kissing, even to this day. Sounds a bit strange, but it's true. As one woman recently wrote, "We used to take kissing for granted, but no more." That's because study after study reveals the good that comes from a kiss between husband and wife.

For example, did you know that those who kiss their loved one each morning miss less work because of illness than those who do not? Those who kiss have fewer auto accidents on the way to work. They earn twenty to thirty percent more monthly and live approximately five years longer. And if that weren't enough, scientists have also found that kissing produces a hormone in our brain that elevates our mood. So pucker up and don't neglect kissing as a terrific way to meet your daily requirement of touch.

A Final Thought on Touching Your Spouse

The value of human touch is almost incalculable. Studies have shown it to be an asset for calming anxiety, alleviating stress, and treating arthritis, back pain, cancer, blood pressure, depression, headaches, and on and on. A study at UCLA estimated that if some type-A driven men would hug their wives several times each day, it would increase their life span by almost two years, not to mention the way it would improve their marriages. That same study reported that eight to ten meaningful touches each day help us maintain emotional and physical health. It's indisputable. So why not take advantage of this gift that is built right into your marriage—the relationship that provides the opportunity for more touch than any other.

In fact, of the couples we interviewed about this important quality, they mentioned one behavior more than any other that has helped them include touching on a daily basis: holding hands. Remember doing that? If you've been married a few years, you may have forgotten this little gem. So simple. So easy. Why is it that so many married couples no longer hold hands? Probably doesn't matter why. What does matter is that you not lose touch (pardon the pun) with this trademark method of connecting. It could very well be one of the most important things you do all day.

For Reflection

1. How did your parents and family show affection? Do you like or dislike the kind of physical affection you grew up with?

2. What kind of touch do you like most?

3. When do you like to be touched? When do you not like to be touched?

4. How can you greet each other more affectionately at the end of the day?

5. I like to be kissed. . . (fill in the blank)

6. I like to be hugged . . . (fill in the blank)

7. How can you incorporate more touch into your life?

Once a Day . . .

FIND SOMETHING THAT MAKES YOU BOTH LAUGH

The most wasted of all days is one without laughter.

E. E. CUMMINGS

Do you two need a tissue?" a voice gently whispered from behind us. We were sitting in a quiet theater watching a somber play when—at the saddest moment—something struck us as funny. Hysterically funny.

At just that moment, Les found a withered old banana in his coat pocket. Who knows how long it had lived there. He set this surprising discovery on my knee. Caught off guard by the incongruity of the banana and the play, I developed one of the worst cases of the giggles I've ever had. Les quickly caught the same disease. We tried desperately to stifle our laughter, but, as we bowed our heads to hide our faces, we couldn't keep our shoulders from shuddering. An older woman behind us, thinking we were moved by what was happening on stage, offered us a tissue for our tears, which made us want to laugh all the more. When Les accepted her kind offer, I really lost it and had to leave the theater.

Just another day in the marriage of Les and Leslie? Not quite, but we do laugh a lot together. The tiniest of things can sometimes set us off—a slight inflection or a knowing glance, for example. We can quote a funny line from a movie or sitcom for weeks. Better still are the unplanned faux pas in front of others that bring embarrassment. We have the same funny bone and can't keep from using it. No wonder we enjoy our marriage.

Laughter bonds people. Any good friend will tell you that laughter is the shortest distance between two people—especially in marriage. But one never knows what's funny to others. In a survey of over fourteen thousand *Psychology Today* readers who rated thirty jokes, the findings were unequivocal. "Every single joke," it was reported, "had a substantial number of fans who rated it 'very funny,' while another group dismissed it as 'not at all funny.'" Apparently, our funny bones are located in different places. Some laugh uproariously at the slapstick of Larry, Moe, and Curly-Joe, while others enjoy the more cerebral humor of Woody Allen.

Wherever you are on this continuum of humor, one thing is certain: Laughter, on a daily basis, is like taking a vitamin for your marriage. And it is a healthy habit all loving couples enjoy.

Why Laughter Is Good for Your Marriage

Laughter is good medicine, literally. It has important physiological effects on you and your soul mate. The French philosopher Voltaire wrote, "The art of medicine consists of amusing the patient while nature cures the disease." Modern research indicates that people with a sense of humor have fewer symptoms of physical illness than those who are less humorous. This idea, of course, isn't new. Since King

Solomon's time, people have known about and applied the healing benefits of humor. As Proverbs tells us, "A cheerful heart is good medicine" (17:22).

But humor brings more than physiological benefits to a husband and wife. Humor helps us cope. Consider Janet, who wanted to impress a small group of couples with an elaborate dinner. She cooked all day and enlisted her husband's help to serve the meal. All went well until the main course. As her husband was bringing in the crown roast, the kitchen door hit him from behind and the platter flew across the room. Janet froze, regained her composure, then commanded, "Dear, don't just stand there. Pick up the roast, go in the kitchen, and get the *other* one!"

No doubt about it, humor helps us cope—not just with the trivial but even with the tragic. Psychoanalyst Martin Grotjahn, author of *Beyond Laughter*, notes that "to have a sense of humor is to have an understanding of human suffering." Charlie Chaplin could have said the same thing. Chaplin grew up in the poorest section of London. His mother suffered from serious mental illness and his father died of alcoholism when Charlie was just five. Laughter was Chaplin's tool for coping with life's losses. Chaplin eating a boiled leather shoe for dinner in his classic film *Gold Rush* is more than a humorous scene. It is an act of human triumph, a monument to the coping power of humor.

One does not need to be a professional comedian, however, to benefit from comedy. Viktor Frankl is another example of how humor can empower a person to contend with horrendous circumstances. In Frankl's book *Man's Search for Meaning*, he speaks of using humor to survive imprisonment during World

Assessing Your Funny Factor

So how's your funny bone? Heard any good jokes lately? The following self-test will help you measure how much humor you are bringing into your marriage. So take a moment, individually, to answer these questions as honestly as you can, then compare your answers with each other.

T   F   I have a fail-safe strategy to make my partner laugh and it almost always works.

T   F   Since humor can sometimes backfire, I'm pretty good at knowing the moments when I should avoid it.

T   F   I can remember something specific we both laughed about yesterday.

T   F   We have several inside jokes that few people would understand.

T   F   I'd say we laugh together more than most couples do.

T   F   While I know to be careful, I feel safe poking fun at my spouse on occasion.

T   F   If asked to describe my partner's sense of humor, I'd have a pretty good understanding of it.

T   F   I sometimes make fun of myself to make my spouse laugh.

T   F   I use humor (very carefully) on occasion to defuse a tense moment between us.

T   F   We often recount humorous incidents we've experienced, days after they've occurred.

Add up the number of "true" responses. If it is eight or higher, you are well on your way to enjoying a daily dose of humor. If your score isn't that high, you will certainly benefit from the tips we offer in this chapter for finding something to laugh about each day as a couple.

War II. Frankl and another inmate would invent at least one amusing story daily to help them cope with their horrors.

A Nazi prison camp is a dramatic backdrop to underscore the value of humor, but it may help you remember what a good laugh can do for you and your marriage on stressful days. Let's be honest, every marriage has its difficulties. When the checkbook doesn't balance, when the kids can't seem to behave, when busy schedules collide, when you can't remember your last date-night, not to mention your last vacation. For these times, and dozens of others, humor is invaluable. Take it from the professionals: Legendary comedian Bob Hope says laughter is an "instant vacation." Jay Leno says, "You can't stay mad at somebody who makes you laugh." And the great Bill Cosby says, "If you can find humor in anything, you can survive it." Researchers agree. Studies reveal that individuals who have a strong sense of humor are less likely to experience burnout and depression and they are more likely to enjoy life in general—including their marriage.

Bringing a Daily Dose of Laughter into Your Marriage

Essayist and biographer Agnes Repplier, who was known for her common sense and good judgment, said, "We cannot really love anybody with whom we never laugh." We couldn't agree more. And we believe the implication of her statement is also true: The more you laugh together, the more you love your spouse. So, with this in mind, we offer the following tips on bringing a daily dose of laughter into your marriage.

Remember rule number 6.

Two prime ministers are sitting in a room discussing affairs of state. Suddenly a man bursts in shouting and stamping and banging his fist on the desk. The resident prime minister admonishes him. "Peter," he says, "kindly remember rule number 6," whereupon Peter is instantly restored to complete calm, apologizes, and withdraws. The politicians return to their conversation, only to be interrupted yet again twenty minutes later by a hysterical woman gesticulating wildly, her hair flying. Again the intruder is greeted with the words "Marie, please remember rule number 6." Complete calm descends once more, and she too withdraws with a bow and an apology.

When the scene is repeated a third time, the visiting prime minister addresses his colleague: "My dear friend, I've seen many things in my life, but never anything as remarkable as this. Would you be willing to share with me the secret of rule number 6?"

"Very simple," replies the resident prime minister. "Rule number 6 is 'Don't take yourself so seriously.'"

"Ah," says his visitor, "that is a fine rule." After a moment of pondering, he inquires, "And what, may I ask, are the other rules?"

"There aren't any."

Rule number 6 is a good rule for every spouse who's looking for a daily dose of laughter. If you're like most people, you can take life and yourself a little too seriously, and that always stunts laughter. So lighten up. Relax. Remember what really matters. And remember rule number 6.

Poke fun at your spouse—carefully.

In college I (Leslie) shared a single bathroom with several other girls on the same floor of a residence hall. I enjoyed communal living during that time of my life. We all became good friends and learned so much about each other—especially each other's little quirks. One of the girls, for example, was often irritated by the little globs of toothpaste that inevitably appeared in the bathroom sink each morning from so many users. Everyone knew Lisa would complain. We came to expect it and often joked with her about being a neat-freak.

When Lisa got married at the end of our school year, we were all at her wedding, and one of us (who shall remain nameless) warned her soon-to-be husband about her dislike of toothpaste in the sink. Apparently, he made a mental note of the comment, and when Lisa went into the bathroom on the first morning of their honeymoon, she found the following message written in the sink with a thick blue line of toothpaste: "I Love You, Lisa!"

This new husband understood the value of a good marital laugh right from the beginning. And while his first attempt at poking fun at his wife could have backfired, it didn't. To this day, years later, they both love telling the story.

Now, let's be clear that poking fun at your spouse must be done with caution. For example, you should steer clear of joking about sensitive issues, such as your partner's weight, family, work, and so on. In other words, if you're not sure if your partner will think it's funny, you'd better refrain.

Laugh when you don't feel like laughing.

A woman discovered a shelf of reduced-price items at a local bookstore. Among the gifts was a little figurine of a man and woman, their heads lovingly tilted toward one another. "Happy 10th Anniversary" read the inscription. It appeared to be in perfect condition, yet its tag indicated "damaged." Examining it more closely, she found another tag underneath that read "Wife is coming unglued."

Let's face it, no spouse is immune to stress. We all feel like we're coming unglued at times. And wise experts agree that the best way for anyone to cope is with a good laugh. "Humor makes all things tolerable," said preacher Henry Ward Beecher. "Laugh out loud," says Chuck Swindoll. "It helps flush out the nervous system." On another occasion Chuck said, "Laughter is the most beautiful and beneficial therapy God ever granted humanity." Arnold Glasgow said, "Laughter is a tranquilizer with no side effects." The point is that even when you've had a tough day, or should we say *especially* when you've had a tough day, you need to laugh. It will help wash away the stress and keep the two of you together when you're coming unglued. So help each other to find something funny even when it's not easy.

Look for the funny around you.

On a recent flight between Seattle and Oklahoma City, I (Leslie) had my head buried in a book and was oblivious to my husband's boredom. He had nothing to read, and in his desperation, he began thumbing through in-flight magazines. Unbeknownst to me, Les was cutting various pictures out of these magazines with his handy Swiss Army pocket knife (this was before such a gizmo would be confiscated by airport security). He found a large photo of a monkey head and placed it in the window next to his seat. He cut out the watch from a photo advertisement for Rolex and taped it to his wrist. And to top off his cutting spree, he found a red ball and taped it to his nose.

Knowing that timing is everything when it comes to humor, Les waited. We sat side by side in our cramped little seats, and he waited. I read. He waited. Les waited for me to look up from my book so he could see my reaction to a monkey looking in on us at thirty-five hundred feet. He waited for me to ask for the time so he could see me react to his "Rolex." He waited to see the reaction I'd have to a clown nose taped to the somber face of my husband. Les waited so long—he fell asleep. But that didn't spoil the fun.

When I finally looked up from my book, I saw his handiwork. But I muffled my laughter to let him enjoy his sleep. In fact, I decided to take a catnap too. Who knows how long we slept, but it was long enough for two flight attendants to don red noses and wake us up to tell us we were landing.

You never know where you can find a good laugh. So look for the funny around you and create it when you have to.

Study your spouse's funny bone.

One of the reasons many couples never reach their "laughter potential" is because they have never taken humor seriously. Sounds strange, but to bring more laughter into your relationship, you need to know what makes your husband or wife laugh. After all, each of us has a unique sense of humor.

As public speakers, we've experienced occasions where someone will laugh out loud at something most everyone else would barely chuckle at. And, of course, some people never crack a smile at something almost everyone else thinks is hilarious. So your job is to find those things your partner thinks are most funny by paying attention to when he or she laughs.

"I never realized how much Susan laughs at a silly comic strip," a participant at one of our seminars told us. "When you asked us to think about each other's humor styles, it dawned on me that I hardly ever laugh at comics in the paper, but she seems to really enjoy them." This enlightened husband went on to tell us how he was now learning to laugh at comic strips too. He now makes a habit out of reading them and even cuts one out to show Susan from time to time.

Maybe your partner likes a sarcastic wit. Maybe it's slapstick that makes him or her laugh. Or maybe it's the old classic sitcoms like *The Andy Griffith Show*. Wherever his or her funny bone is located, find it and use it—at least once a day.

A Final Thought on Humor

The healing power of laughter was not taken seriously by the scientific world until the late Norman Cousins, former editor of *Saturday Review* and subsequently professor at UCLA's School of Medicine, wrote about his life-changing experience with humor. As he reported in his book *Anatomy of an Illness*, laughter helped turn the tide of a serious collagen disease. "I made the joyous discovery," Cousins reported, "that ten minutes of genuine belly laughter had an anesthetic effect and would give me at least two hours of pain-free sleep." He surrounded himself with Marx Brothers films and *Candid Camera* videos. He also checked out of the hospital and moved into a hotel where, as he says, he could "laugh twice as hard at half the price."

Cousins called laughter "inner jogging" because every system in our body gets a workout when we have a hearty laugh. Laboratory studies support Cousins' hunches. Our cardiovascular and respiratory systems, for example, benefit more from twenty seconds of robust laughter than from three minutes of exercise on a rowing machine. Through laughter, muscles release tension and neurochemicals are released into the bloodstream, creating the same feelings that long-distance joggers experience as "runner's high."

So, lighten up. Learning to laugh a little more just may save you life, not to mention your marriage. To paraphrase Henry Ward Beecher, "A marriage without a sense of humor is like a wagon without springs—jolted by every pebble in the road."

For Reflection

1. How would you describe you and your partner's funny bones? In other words, what makes each of you laugh?

2. Have you ever found yourselves laughing at something that nobody else thinks is funny? What do those moments reveal about your shared humor?

3. Are you more likely to laugh at Jay Leno or David Letterman? Why?

4. Recall a time when humor backfired in your marriage. What happened and what can you learn from it?

5. How can you incorporate more humor into your married life?

Once a Week...

Anybody can observe the Sabbath, but making it holy surely takes the rest of the week.

ALICE WALKER

Once a Week ...

DO SOMETHING ACTIVE
THAT LIFTS YOUR SPIRITS

> *Spending recreational time with his wife is second only to sex for the typical husband.*
>
> WILLARD F. HARLEY JR.

One crisp autumn day Tom asked Kelly to a Kansas City Chiefs game. "That sounds great! What time?" Kelly said. They made the date, and Tom smiled after he hung up. This was their third date in the last four weeks, and he was so pleased that she sounded eager to go to a football game.

Tom and Kelly had a great time at the game and took in several more games that same season. They also shopped for cars. Not because either of them needed one. Tom simply enjoyed studying the latest models, and Kelly seemed to enjoy it too. Their relationship was getting more serious, and Tom felt so fortunate to find a woman who enjoyed the same things he did.

By mid-winter, Tom was certain Kelly was the woman for him. They got married that spring, and both were in bliss. But sometime during their first married year, Kelly's interest in football lessened. She and Tom would sometimes watch the Monday night games, but she never got too excited about attending one. And when Tom suggested that they go to an upcoming automobile show, Kelly begged off.

"I thought you liked looking at cars," Tom complained.

"Oh, honey, I do. I guess I just don't enjoy it as much as you do," Kelly said.

That came as a surprise to Tom. Over the next year, Tom discovered that the things he liked to do and the things Kelly liked to do had little in common. Gradually they arrived at the point where they rarely did much together except go out to dinner once in a while. Tom would have preferred to spend more "fun" time with Kelly, but she seemed quite content to let him do his own thing. Hurt and bewildered, Tom often wondered why his wife didn't want to be with him.

One of the great gaps between husbands and wives is in their notions of emotional intimacy. If you are like most women, intimacy means sharing secrets, talking things over, cuddling, and so on. But a man builds intimacy differently. He connects by *doing* things together. Working in the garden or going to a movie with his wife gives him a feeling of closeness.

Husbands place surprising importance on having their wives as recreational companions. The commercial caricature of men out in the wilderness, cold beer in hand, saying, "It doesn't get any better than this," is false. It can get a lot better than that when a wife joins her husband in a shared activity they both enjoy.

That's why in this chapter we encourage you to do something active together that lifts your spirits. Put it on your to-do list this week and every week. If you're already worried that you can't find something in common that you'll both enjoy, that's okay. We're going to show you how to do just that.

Why Shared Activity Is Good for Your Marriage

I (Les) had a fantasy about married life that took a while to shake. For whatever reason, I thought Leslie and I would play tennis. I'm not sure why, but I thought this would be an activity we could do together through the years of our marriage. In fact, a few months after we married and moved from Chicago to Los Angeles to go to graduate school, I signed us up for a membership at a local tennis club that gave discounts to students. We bought new racquets, put on our whites, and headed for the courts.

I cracked open a fresh can of balls and lobbed one over the net to Leslie. "Whoa," Leslie hollered, "you're going to have to serve it a lot slower than that." *Slower? She's got to be kidding*, I thought to myself. *Besides that, I'm not even serving.* I tossed another one right to her. Swing and a miss. "Are you okay?" I asked.

"Sure, this is fun," she replied.

Fun for whom? Not me. And, as Leslie later confessed, it wasn't fun for her either. It was one of our earliest lessons in how a good idea for a shared activity can go bad. We've since worked hard to find other activities we enjoy doing together. Most weeks, for example, you will find us working out together at the gym. And most weeks, when Seattle weather permits, you'll find us taking a three-mile walk around Green Lake. And when that doesn't happen, you might find us going to the movies or maybe working in our backyard. We never got the tennis thing worked out, but we've never given up on doing something once a week that gives us both a lift. Why? Because there is too much at stake.

Did you know that passion and intimacy plummet when a spouse associates his or her partner primarily with dirty clothes thoughtlessly dropped on the floor, barked out orders, crying, or nagging? No surprise, right? But so many couples ignore this fact. He plays golf with his buddies. She attends her book club with her friends. They both may keep plenty active, but these activities are too often segregated. And when that's the case, couples miss out on a weekly habit that will buoy their marriage more than they ever imagined. Shared activity is one of the supreme gifts of married life, and it is an insurance policy against the fading of passion and intimacy.

How to Do Something You Both Enjoy

Okay, so you've determined your marriage can benefit from a little more activity together. Your schedule is already jam-packed, and you're not even sure how you'll squeeze in an activity if you find one. Well, here's our best advice, and we've seen it help countless couples cultivate this important habit into their weekly schedule.

Broaden your sphere of interest.

We've counseled enough couples to know you might be saying, "What do you do if you have few activities you like to do together?" The answer: Cultivate your spheres of interest. Don't allow you and your partner to drift apart because you can't find something enjoyable to do together. We have seen too many marriages fizzle because a couple didn't use their creative energies to build enjoyable moments of fun and relaxation together.

Assessing Your Activity Quotient

So how are you doing when it comes to being active together? Are you finding it hard to come up with ideas, or are you feeling pretty content? The following self-test will help you answer these questions. So take a moment, individually, to answer these questions as honestly as you can, then compare your answers with each other.

T F I have learned to enjoy new activities because my spouse enjoys them.

T F We have a specific time reserved on our weekly calendar where we can enjoy doing something together—just the two of us.

T F I know that my partner thoroughly enjoys my company on outings we share.

T F If we don't do something active together during the week, we notice the negative impact on our relationship.

T F One of us has forgone another opportunity to be together for a date.

T F We sometimes take a walk or even a drive just for the fun of being together.

T F I can remember a specific activity we enjoyed doing together last week that lifted our spirits.

T F We rarely run out of ideas of things we'd like to do together.

T F Our friends know what kinds of things we do as a couple.

T F When it comes to doing something active together, we are very creative.

Add up the number of "true" responses. If it is eight or higher, you are well on your way to enjoying the habit of having shared activities in your marriage. Count yourselves blessed. If your score isn't that high, however, you will certainly benefit from the tips we offer in this chapter for finding something to do together as a couple.

So let's get practical. Make a careful list of recreational interests your spouse enjoys. Here are a few to get you started: antique collecting, tennis, racquetball, camping, canoeing, table games, puzzles, cooking, dancing, hiking, horseback riding, jogging, going to a lecture, art gallery, museum, movie-going, ice-skating, downhill skiing, cross-country skiing, sailing, listening to music, swimming, traveling, walking, woodworking, hitting a bucket of balls, and lifting weights. Your list should be as long as possible. Next, circle those activities you might find somewhat pleasurable. You can probably find a good half-dozen activities you can enjoy with your spouse. Your next task is to schedule these activities into your recreational time together.

Make time.

All the good intentions a marriage can muster will never replace the actual doing of the activity together. And the first step toward making that happen is to make time for it. Marriage expert David Mace said, "Love must be fed and nurtured . . . first and foremost it demands time." How true. Studies indicate that marital happiness is highly correlated with the amount of time spent together. So, right now, get your Day-Timers out and find a slot of time the two of you can call your own. It's that simple. Enough said.

Recognize what you bring to the picture (especially as a wife).

Les recently came home from a speaking engagement in Lake Tahoe. Before he left, he was excited because he was going to fly in a day early and do some skiing on his own. I was so happy for him. He loves to ski—fast—and when we go together I always feel like I'm slowing him down. But when he came home from his trip, I was shocked by his report. "Well, the powder was great, and the weather was perfect, but it's just not the same as skiing with you." Wow! All this time I thought I was a tagalong, and it turns out that he doesn't really enjoy skiing without me.

So take it from me as a wife who now knows, your presence means more to your husband than you may think. Don't be inhibited by some self-imposed limitation.

Don't push too hard.

It's Saturday morning as Jake, an avid hunter, wakes up ready to go bag the first deer of the season. He walks down to the kitchen to get a cup of coffee, and to his surprise he finds his wife, Alice, sitting there, fully dressed in camouflage.

Jake asks her, "What are you up to?"

Alice smiles. "I'm going hunting with you!"

Jake, though he has many reservations about this, reluctantly decides to take her along. Later they arrive at the hunting site. Jake sets his wife safely up in the tree stand and tells her, "If you see a deer, take careful aim at it, and I'll come running back as soon as I hear the shot."

Jake walks away with a smile on his face knowing that Alice couldn't bag an elephant—much less a deer. Not ten minutes pass when he is startled as he hears an array of gunshots.

Quickly, Jake starts running back. As Jake gets closer to her stand, he hears Alice screaming, "Get away from my deer!" Confused, Jake races faster toward his screaming wife. And again he hears her yell, "Get away from my deer!" followed by another volley of gunfire. Now within sight of where he had left his wife, Jake is surprised to see a cowboy, with his hands high in the air.

The cowboy, obviously distraught, says, "Okay, lady, okay! You can have your deer! Just let me get my saddle off it!"

Some activities were never really designed to be enjoyed as husband and wife. So give your mate space to enjoy certain activities that are his or hers alone. If your wife likes to work in "her" garden by herself, let her. If your husband wants to golf with his buddies, allow it. As you are finding things to do together, you don't have to change the things you enjoy separately. As the saying goes, couples can share separateness in their togetherness.

Do something crazy.

Some friends told us about a creative couple they know who is always doing something just for fun. Once they went to the airport to find the first flight that was about to take off. Neither had a ticket or even cared where the flight was headed. But they ran to that gate and kissed each other like one of them was leaving for a long good-bye. Once the flight was boarded, they then looked for the next flight about to take off, ran to that gate, and kissed again.

Crazy? Of course. Would we do it? Probably not, especially not in an age of heightened airport security! But it worked for them. They died laughing and had a fun time smooching in the process. And you can bet this couple is never bored. Not a bad lesson: If you're having a tough time coming up with a shared activity this week, try something radical. Come up with an outing that might push your limits.

Brace yourself for change.

As couples learn to cultivate shared activity, it can be a bit jolting, especially if you've been married awhile and this kind of thing is new to your marriage. After all, change is never easy. Take the configuration of the letters on a computer keyboard as an illustration. Back in the 1870s, a manufacturer of typewriters received complaints about the typewriter keys sticking together if the user went too fast. Engineers for the company decided that the best way to keep the keys from jamming was to slow the operator down. So they developed a more inefficient keyboard with letters like "O" and "I" (two of the most frequently used letters in the alphabet) positioned for the relatively weaker ring and little fingers. Depressing these keys simply took more time. The problem was solved—no more jammed keys.

Since the time of that solution, however, typing technology and word processing have advanced significantly. Today's word processors can go much faster than any human can type. The problem is that we don't want to change the keyboard—even though it would help us type faster.

Change is hard (just recall how well the United States assimilated to the metric system), especially when it hits home. But don't allow that to stand in the way of trying to do something new in your marriage. Finding a shared activity can be a challenge for some couples, but a little change can do you good.

A Final Thought on Shared Activity

We've worked with numerous couples in our counseling office to help them cultivate the weekly habit of doing something that lifts their spirits. And every so often we meet a couple who can't seem to find an activity that works. They do everything from bowling to gardening, from table games to rock climbing. And nothing seems to click. If you fall into this camp, we want to encourage you to not give up. Keep exploring. And in the meantime we have two specific suggestions for activities that may get you going.

When all else fails, try this: walking or driving. Countless couples benefit from a simple walk around their neighborhood or a nearby park. Or if walking isn't your thing, a Sunday drive can serve the same purpose. It can become a ritual that allows your collective soul to catch up. It may be long or short, but it is almost guaranteed to bring you together. Of course, this is not the time to complain about something or dump a to-do list on your partner. The goal is to make it a pleasurable time that lifts your burdens simply because you are in each other's company. And if you need a verse to become your motto, we know of no better one that Amos 3:3: "Do two walk together unless they have agreed to do so?" Walking (or driving) puts you on the path of harmony and renewed energy together.

For Reflection

1. *How would sharing an activity together each week bring the two of you closer together?*

2. *Which of the following activities have potential to be shared with your spouse?*

Physical Activities	Events to Attend	Other
Biking	Church events	Card playing
Bird watching	Concerts	Cooking
Boating	Conferences	Collecting
Camping	Conventions	Eating out
Canoeing	Dances	Historical reenactments
Dancing	Lectures	House renovating
Gardening	Movies	Listening to music
Golfing	Musicals	Museum-going
Hiking	Operas	Photography
Horseback riding	Plays	Puzzles
Ice-skating or rollerblading	Sporting events	Shopping
Jogging	Readings	Table games
Swimming	Travelogues	Traveling
Tennis	Volunteering	
Working out	Woodworking	

3. *Of course the above is just to get you started. What other activities might the two of you share together?*

4. *Once you identify a potential shared activity, what will it take for the two of you to actually follow through and do it? Will you need a baby-sitter? Equipment? Get specific.*

Once a Week . . .

BOOST YOUR PARTNER'S
SELF-ESTEEM

> *I can live two months on one compliment.*
>
> MARK TWAIN

In the summer of 1965, a thirteen-and-a-half-foot boat quietly slipped out of the marina at Falmouth, Massachusetts. Its destination? Falmouth, England. It would be the smallest craft ever to make the voyage. Its name? *Tinkerbelle.* Its pilot? Robert Manry, a copy editor for the *Cleveland Plain Dealer,* who felt ten years at the desk was enough boredom for a while, so he took a leave of absence to fulfill his secret dream.

Manry was afraid, not of the ocean, but of all those people who would try to talk him out of the trip. So he didn't share it with many, just some relatives and his wife, Virginia. She was his greatest source of support.

The trip? Anything but pleasant. He spent sleepless nights trying to cross shipping lanes without getting run down and sunk. Weeks at sea caused his food to become tasteless. Loneliness, that age-old monster of the deep, led to terrifying hallucinations. His rudder broke three times. Storms swept him overboard, and had it not been for the rope he had knotted around his waist, he would never have been able to pull himself back on board. Finally, after seventy-eight days alone at sea, he sailed into Falmouth, England.

During those nights at the tiller, he had fantasized about what he would do once he arrived. He expected simply to check into a hotel, eat dinner alone, then the next morning see if, perhaps, the Associated Press might be interested in his story. Was he in for a surprise!

Word of his approach had spread far and wide. To his amazement, three hundred vessels, with horns blasting, escorted *Tinkerbelle* into port. Forty thousand people stood screaming and cheering him to shore. Robert Manry, copy editor turned dreamer, became an overnight hero.

His story has been told around the world. But Robert couldn't have done it alone. Standing on the dock was an even greater hero: Virginia. Refusing to be a passive observer when Robert's dream was taking shape, she not only allowed him freedom to pursue it but encouraged him all along the way. She was her husband's inspiration. She was his number-one cheerleader. She made it possible, and Robert was the first to admit it.

That's the power of a positive spouse. When your soul mate helps you reach your potential, when he or she boosts your self-confidence, your options seem limitless. So among the healthy habits of loving couples, boosting your partner's self-esteem is one of the most prized.

Why Your Partner's Self-Esteem Impacts Your Marriage

Without honing this healthy habit of building up our partner's confidence, we are prone to a deadly alternative. Consider the following news story as an illustration. "Gear Blamed in Crash That Killed Senator" read the headline in the April 29, 1992, issue of the *Chicago Tribune*. "A stripped gear in the propeller controls of a commuter plane caused it to nose-dive into the Georgia woods last April, killing former U.S. Senator John Tower of Texas and 22 others, the government concluded Tuesday." The story went on to say, "A gear that adjusted the pitch of the left engine's propellers was slowly worn away by an opposing part with a harder titanium coating." According to the National Transportation Safety Board, "It acted like a file, and over time it wore down the teeth that controlled the propeller."

As we pondered this sad story and how one single gear could create such tragedy, we realized that the titanium-coated gear that wore away the softer gear is similar to a spouse who wears away the spirit of his or her partner. Week after week, month after month, and year after year, an abrasive spouse erodes the self-concept of even the healthiest of partners. It's impossible to live with another person and not be impacted by his or her words—whether they be positive or negative.

Of course, the detrimental impact of negative words is obvious. Every decent husband or wife steers clear of this as best they can. But that's not enough. We humans cannot survive with only the absence of the negative; we require a regular diet of the positive. Without it our spirit—and thus our marriage—withers. As Celeste Holm so aptly put it, "We live by encouragement and die without it—slowly, sadly, angrily." This is reason enough to make this habit a part of each week!

Encouragement is perhaps the finest gift we ever give our spouse. The words used to build spouses up are the fuel taking them to their full potential. Sydney Madwed said, "If everyone received the encouragement they need to grow, the genius in most everyone would blossom and the world would produce

Assessing How Well You Stroke Your Mate's Ego

So how are you doing when it comes to encouraging your spouse? Does he or she have a higher level of self-esteem because of you? The following self-test will help you answer these questions. So take a moment, individually, to answer these questions as honestly as you can, then compare your answers with each other.

T F   I can almost always find something to praise my partner for.

T F   I give my partner twice as many positive comments in a given week than I do negative ones.

T F   I am confident that my spouse feels encouraged and affirmed by me.

T F   When my spouse has a new idea that isn't initially to my liking, I refrain from judgment and listen with an open mind.

T F   I honestly admire my spouse.

T F   I can recall a specific incident within the last week where I deliberately praised my partner.

T F   My spouse is not defensive.

T F   I tell my partner how much I appreciate him or her even when I think he or she already knows it.

T F   My spouse could immediately name one specific thing I've affirmed him or her for in the past seven days.

T F   I can't remember a time within the past several days where I said something critical to my partner about his or her behavior.

Add up the number of "true" responses. If it is eight or higher, you can pat yourself on the back for doing a good job of encouraging and praising your partner. If your score isn't that high, however, you will certainly benefit from the tips we offer in this chapter for finding creative ways of instilling this healthy habit.

abundance beyond the wildest dreams. We would have more than one Einstein, Edison, Schweitzer, Mother Teresa, Dr. Salk, and other great minds in a century."

Whether that be true or not, one thing is certain. Encouragement is sure to help your marriage run more smoothly. It lowers your spouse's defenses. It makes meaningful connections more common. It sets the stage for a better sex life. And on and on. It is difficult to exaggerate the value of this healthy habit.

How to Boost Your Partner's Self-Esteem

If you're feeling like your ability to boost your mate's self-esteem could use a boost itself, we have plenty of suggestions. Below are some practical and proven ways to encourage your spouse.

Be prepared for shock.

A man accompanied his friend home for dinner and was impressed by the way he entered his house, asked his wife how her day went, and told her she looked pretty. Then, when they'd embraced, she served dinner. After they ate, the husband complimented his wife on the meal and thanked her for it. When the two fellows were alone, the visitor asked, "Why do you treat your wife so well?"

"Because she deserves it, and it makes our marriage happier," replied the host.

Impressed, the visitor decided to adopt the idea. Arriving home, he embraced his wife and exclaimed, "You look wonderful!" For good measure he added, "Sweetheart, I'm the luckiest guy in the world."

His wife, amazed, burst into tears. Bewildered, he asked her, "What in the world's the matter?"

She wept, "What a day! Billy fought at school. The refrigerator quit and spoiled the groceries. And now you come home drunk!"

We chuckle, yet sadly, this joke reflects a good many marriages. If we've had a long dry spell without encouragement, we may be flat-out shocked that our spouse would say a positive word. So if that's the case in your relationship, do your best to accept the praise without making him or her feel like a heel for not saying it sooner.

Look for diamonds.

A twenty-five–year study involving fourteen thousand families recently uncovered a secret to building a stronger family. Successful families—those that avoid the daily dissension that often leads to fractured relationships—build a wall of appreciation and encouragement around themselves, according to the research team at the University of Alabama in Tuscaloosa. "Strong families are good diamond hunters," according to Nick Stinnett, lead researcher and professor of human development at the university. "They dig through the rough looking for the good in each other. They build each other psychologically and realize that the need to be appreciated is one of the deepest needs we all have." And if that's true for the whole family, it certainly applies to the marriage, so start looking for diamonds by calling attention to the things you genuinely appreciate about your spouse.

Uncover your spouse's sweet spot of praise.

If you want this healthy habit to make a difference, you're going to need to accurately understand what makes your spouse feel affirmed. It's not enough to toss out compliments. "Great meal, honey" isn't going to cut it. Of course, you don't want to give that up, but you're going to need to go deeper. What is it that your spouse really wants to hear from you? Is it that she's a good cook? Maybe. Is it that he's good at mowing the lawn? Maybe. But maybe your spouse is yearning to hear something else. Maybe she wants to know that you admire the way she volunteers to help in the nursery at church or her gift for organizing your home. Maybe he's dying to be noticed for how he interacts with the children or how he provides financial security for your family.

The things you praise in your partner may be things that don't matter as much to him or her as others. She may feel quite confident in her cooking ability but more insecure about the good she does as a volunteer. He may not give a rip about his lawn work, but he takes great pride in being a good father.

The most meaningful admiration in your marriage will come from a sincere heart that notices what really matters—what your partner really values. So ask yourself what he or she feels most insecure about. And discover what he or she values. That is your partner's sweet spot of praise. And the more you compliment it, the more you admire it, the more on target this healthy habit will be.

Pay attention to the four legs of self-esteem.

In his helpful book *That's Not What I Meant!* Tim Stafford notes that our self-esteem stands on four legs: mental, social, physical, and spiritual. People need to feel capable mentally, likable socially, attractive physically, and vital spiritually.

Stafford points out that we need praise in each of these areas from our partner.

Your spouse wants to feel intellectually competent around you. He or she wants to know you recognize his or her sharp thinking. This is especially true if your spouse is often affirmed more in other areas. If she is often complimented on her appearance, for example, it is especially important that you recognize her mental abilities. Say things like, "I like the way you think," or, "You are so good at conceptualizing a problem," or, "You are really smart in that area."

Likewise, we all want to feel physically attractive—especially to our spouse. To boost up this area, say things like, "You look handsome in that shirt," or, "I'm still knocked out by your smile," or, "I like watching you move."

When it comes to social abilities, your spouse needs to know you respect him or her here too. And they feel it most when you say things like, "You're a good listener," or, "You know just how I feel," or, "I love hearing your voice on the phone."

And don't neglect your spouse's spiritual life. She needs to know you value how she relates to God. This comes through when you say things like, "I can see how you really depend on God," or, "I admire how faithful you are studying your Bible," or, "I look up to you in this area, did you know that?"

Focus on who your spouse is, not only on what he or she does.

We had just stepped onto the platform in the Rose Garden Arena in Portland, Oregon, where nearly fifteen thousand people had assembled for a mega-marriage seminar. That night each of the six speakers was to give a brief overview of what we would be speaking on over the next couple of days. Just before

Leslie and I went to the podium, our friend Gary Smalley captivated the crowd by holding up a crisp fifty-dollar bill and asking the massive audience, "Who would like this fifty-dollar bill?" Hands started going up everywhere. He said, "I am going to give this fifty dollars to one of you, but first let me do this." He proceeded to crumple up the bill. He then asked, "Who still wants it?" The same hands went up in the air.

"Well," he replied, "what if I do this?" He dropped it on the ground and started to grind it into the floor with his shoe. He picked it up, all crumpled and dirty. "Now who still wants it?" Again, hands went into the air.

"You have all learned a valuable lesson," Gary said. "No matter what I did to the money, you still wanted it because it did not decrease in value. It is still worth fifty dollars. Many times in our lives, we are dropped, crumpled, and ground into the dirt by the decisions we make and the circumstances that come our way. We feel as though we are worthless. But no matter what has happened or what will happen, you will never lose your value in God's eyes. Dirty or clean, crumpled or finely creased, you are priceless to him."

Does your spouse need the same lesson that crowd in Portland learned? If so, this healthy habit will be particularly important to your marriage. Your spouse needs to know that your love, as well as God's love, is not dependent on how he looks or what he does.

Make a good list.

This is going to sound elementary and perfunctory, but if you take it seriously, the simple task we are about to give you is sure to pay big marital dividends.

Make a list of a half dozen things you appreciate about your spouse. Literally take the time to ponder this and write them down. It is essential that you be as specific as possible and focus on character traits—not just what he or she does for you. For example, you may appreciate the way your spouse arranges your clean laundry or turns down your bed at night, but the underlining character trait may be that she is thoughtful. You may appreciate that your husband always pays your bills on time, but the character trait may be that he is disciplined. You get the idea. Consider admirable traits such as being compassionate, generous, kind, devout, creative, elegant, honest, affectionate, energetic, gentle, optimistic, committed, faithful, confident, cheerful, and so on. For each character trait you identify, note two or three examples of how you typically notice it in your partner.

Give yourself some time to construct this list, but once you have it, we guarantee you that your spouse would love to see it. In fact, you may want to set aside specific time as a couple to share your lists. Whether or not you do this, however, the real value of this exercise is found by keeping your list handy. Put it in your wallet. Place it on your desk. This will help you again and again in your efforts to boost your partner's self-esteem. As you review your list from time to time, it will help you be more aware of your partner's attributes and far more likely to compliment them.

Steer clear of flattery.

Before you heap words of encouragement and praise on your spouse, we have a big caution. Never do it insincerely. Your spouse has a built-in radar detector for phoniness. He or she knows when you are simply going through the motions, and you will do more harm than good if you simply say flattering words. Praise and admiration must reflect genuine feelings to have any value.

Without sincerity, praise becomes downright annoying and maybe even manipulative. Your wife doesn't want to hear that you think she's beautiful if what you really want is to have sex. And your husband doesn't want to hear how much you admire his skill at fixing things if you have a list of home projects you want him to take on. The bottom line? If you don't mean it, don't say it. Or, if you have an ulterior motive in saying it, keep quiet.

Final Thoughts on Giving and Receiving Praise

We would be remiss if we did not mention two more small bits of information on this healthy habit. First, be sure to accept appreciation gracefully. Some people want to brush it aside or play it down in an attempt to be humble. This never feels good to the person giving the praise. So don't discourage praise by questioning its merit. Instead, say, "Glad you like it," or, "That's kind of you to notice."

Second, become aware of how good it feels to shower your partner in praise. Notice not just what it does for his or her spirit, but what it does for your own. George Burton Adams, an American educator and historian, said it nicely: "Note how good you feel after you have encouraged someone else. No other argument is necessary to suggest that you should never miss the opportunity to give encouragement."

For Reflection

1. Almost everyone struggles with being as affirming and encouraging as they would like. Why do you think it is difficult for so many of us to build up our partner's self-esteem?

2. Recall a time when you felt affirmed and encouraged by your partner. What made it so meaningful and memorable?

3. What is one specific area that you would like your partner to notice more? In other words, where could you use a little more affirmation?

4. Consider how you might devise a mental jogger to help you to remember to boost your partner's self-esteem. Maybe it's when you see him or her at dinner. Maybe it's when you are cleaning up the house. What might it be for you?

Once a Month . . .

> *The development of a really good marriage is not a natural process. It is an achievement.*
>
> DAVID AND VERA MACE

Once a Month . . .

RID YOURSELVES
OF HARMFUL RESIDUE

I believe in opening mail once a month, whether it needs it or not.

BOB CONSIDINE

Of all the seasons, autumn is my (Les's) favorite. Leaves become brilliant. The mornings become crisp and frosty. Firewood is cut. Footballs are thrown. Pumpkins grow bigger. And of course, school begins. I love school (after all, I'm a professor!). Freshly sharpened pencils. A clean stack of notebook paper. The cracking spine of a new textbook. And best of all, a fresh academic start.

It's always nice to have a fresh start—especially when it comes to marriage. And that is exactly what we dedicate this chapter to. Let's face it. Every marriage needs a chance to clear the air. There's enough wear and tear on any given couple living together day in and day out that a monthly meeting to keep things running smoothly should almost be mandatory. Can you imagine the difference it would make?

Compare two couples. Both are traveling at the speed of life: rushing to work in the morning, taking kids to soccer practice, scurrying to get some semblance of a meal together, paying bills, and all the rest. Of course both run into inevitable difficulties, squabbles and spats that flare up and fade. But there is a notable difference between them. Over the years, one of the couples seems increasingly more distant. They used to connect before falling asleep; now she crashes into bed while he stays up to work at his computer. In the past when they went to a party, they'd keep tabs on each other with a knowing glance and even communicate across the room with their own secret code. Nowadays they barely notice each other at a social gathering. They used to read the same books and have lively discussions. They'd share a cup of coffee in the morning. Not these days. Somewhere over the last few years, their meaningful moments have become buried under a mountain of resentment, frustration, bickering, and strife. Every move they make seems to bring up an issue that causes one or the other pain. She sometimes feels like she is walking in a minefield, not knowing what will set him off, and he's still wondering if he can trust her not to blab their personal life to her girlfriends. Do they love each other? Yes. Are they happy with where they've ended up? No.

The other couple, with the same fast pace, running into the same struggles with anger, frustration, hurt feelings, and all the rest, is markedly different. In spite of their turmoil, they still connect. They still share meaningful moments and enjoy each other's company. Sure, they have their meltdowns; they fight. But they don't hold onto their pain and resentment. They've learned to clear the decks and start fresh. How? By being intentional about ridding themselves of harmful residue. They've found a way to release their marriage from all the damaging emotions that would otherwise stick to them and drag on their marriage like barnacles.

You can do the same thing. This chapter will show you how.

Why Ridding Yourselves of Harmful Residue Is Important

When I (Les) was in high school my father had a Buick that he drove hard. Because of his job, he put more miles on his automobiles than most people do. Once he took a car with sixty thousand miles and brought it to a shop that had a sterling reputation for giving extra years to worn-out engines. They literally took the engine and underpinnings of that Buick apart, cleaned up each piece, removed the buildup of any grease and gunk, and handed the keys back to my dad. "We'll want to see it every four months if you want to keep it running this good," the mechanic told him. My dad followed his advice, and the car ran like new until he traded it in at 160,000 miles.

In much the same way, couples can add miles onto their marriage with a regular tune-up. Not only that, they can improve their ride. The practice of ridding your marriage of harmful residue is important because it cleans your system of all the emotional gunk that keeps you from enjoying intimacy at the level you'd like. Harmful residue blocks you from enjoying the level of intimacy that only couples in the top ten percent experience. Stacey Oliker, a sociologist and marriage expert, revealed that the gap between true intimacy and real life remains wide for most married couples. Only a small minority of couples experience genuine intimacy.

Oliker claims that marriage partners seek to fill this gap by being more intimate with close friends than they are with their mates. In *Best Friends and Marriage*, she states that many women, for example, seek out friends or relatives before confiding in their husbands. Similarly, when men were asked to name the person they would most likely talk to about their future dreams and ambitions, close friends outnumbered wives. Why? Because husbands and wives often feel there is too much painful baggage, too much harmful residue for their partners to completely understand them.

The bottom line? If a couple does not routinely clean their relationship of damaging emotions and lingering pain, they are bound to drift apart. They are certain to lose the sense of connectedness that brought them together in the first place.

How to Rid Yourselves of Harmful Residue

This monthly exercise is essential to keeping your relationship fresh and healthy. Just like a beautiful rose bush needs pruning on a regular basis, so your marriage needs to eliminate unnecessary baggage weighing it down. Here we give you some ideas for doing just that. Choose the ones that seem most meaningful to you and set aside an hour or two this month—and every month—where you can pour a couple cups of coffee and tune up your marriage engine.

Explore unfinished business.

One of the reasons many couples have harmful residue building up over the months of their marriage is that they never come to terms with unfinished business. This business may have to do with unpaid bills, a question of how long the

Assessing Your Residue Quotient

So how are you doing when it comes to keeping your relationship fresh and healthy? Do you regularly rid yourselves of harmful residue? The following self-test will help you answer these questions. So take a moment, individually, to answer these questions as honestly as you can, then compare your answers with each other.

T F We have a regular and deliberate time each month when we talk about our marriage to be sure we are in tune.

T F We are good about making decisions and taking action so we are not weighed down by unfinished business.

T F I can't remember the last time I felt lonely.

T F If I purchase a new set of golf clubs or a new dress, I always tell my spouse exactly how much it cost.

T F If I'm feeling particularly anxious or worried about something important to me, I don't expect my spouse to calm my nerves.

T F I rarely erupt with anger, but when I do, we eventually talk calmly about it and move past it.

T F I sense a lot of grace from my spouse. I can make mistakes and still feel accepted by him or her.

T F I can't remember the last time I fibbed to my spouse about how much money I spent on something.

T F I know what is weighing most heavily on my partner's heart this month.

T F We regularly compare our calendars for the coming month and do some advance coordination to make life run more smoothly.

Add up the number of "true" responses. If it is eight or higher, you can rest assured that you are doing an excellent job of keeping your marriage clear of undue obstacles. If your score isn't that high, however, you have a bit of work to do and will certainly benefit from the tips we offer in this chapter for increasing how well you know your spouse.

in-laws are staying for Christmas, whether the kids should be disciplined a certain way, whether you are spending too much time away from the family when you golf, whether to have another baby, and whether you are overextended by singing in the church choir as well as teaching a Sunday school class. Whatever the issue, mark this down: *Every couple has unfinished business.* And that business nags at them. It drags them down and drains them of energy.

In one of the courses we teach at our university, we use a simple illustration to underscore the tension that mounts when business goes unfinished. We play the first three notes of Beethoven's *Fifth Symphony*—noticeably leaving off the fourth note. Then we wait for a student to complete it. Normally it takes about a split second. They quickly get the point. We need closure. We need to have completion. If we don't, we feel unfinished and annoyed.

The same is true in marriage. Every time we have an issue that goes unattended, we increase the pressure and tension in our relationship. So begin your session of ridding yourselves of harmful residue by noting your unfinished business. Talk about whatever it may be, and do your best to make some decisions at this point and gain some closure. To get you started, ask each other: What unfinished business in our relationship is weighing on you most right now?

Talk about feeling alone.

Loneliness—the painful awareness that we are not meaningfully connected to others—floods the lives of millions. And most married people, at some point, believed they had conveniently sidestepped this loathsome feeling simply by getting married. Yet countless spouses, in the same house with their partner, have times of feeling eerily lonely.

Why would a person in a committed, loving relationship feel lonely? The answer may not be what you want to hear, but it's true. Loneliness is often the result of protecting oneself against rejection. Even in marriage, we can erect a wall that prevents our true self from being seen and accepted. We reason that if we are not vulnerable, our partner cannot reject our real selves. Such self-defeating attitudes usually stem from rejection as children. When this is the case, one's ability to trust other people—even a spouse—has been damaged and must be restored.

Rebuilding the kind of trust that diminishes loneliness begins with the courage to risk authenticity. It begins by disclosing your real feelings. That means turning off the television and other distractions to have a meaningful heart-to-heart talk about what's going on with both of you. To get you started, ask each other these questions: When have you felt most lonely in the last thirty days? How can I help lessen that loneliness?

Talk about your money.

The 1960s and 1970s ushered in the sexual revolution where couples cheated and divorce rates soared. Now it's the twenty-first century, and people are still cheating on their spouses. "Only now," according to William Bunch of the *Philadelphia Daily News*, "they're having a secret love affair with Ann Taylor. Or with Eddie Bauer." If you own one of those "priceless" Mastercards, or if you've ever hid receipts in your underwear drawer, then you won't be shocked that the biggest source of lying among married couples isn't sex. It's money.

A *Reader's Digest* survey found the most common lie between spouses is over how much they spent on a purchase. Roughly half, or forty-eight percent, of secretive spouses said they hid the cost of purchases (even in affluent households) within the last month. That was much higher than the two next-most-common secrets, which were over a child's behavior or grades or a failure on the job.

The biggest problem with deceiving your spouse about money is not found in trying to balance the checkbook. No. Money matters are a metaphor for other troubles in a marriage—troubles involving power, security, competence, and self-esteem. That's what makes money so difficult to talk about. And that's why talking about money is vital to this monthly habit of ridding yourselves of harmful residue.

Begin by getting out your checkbook and other records and making a monthly review of where the two of you stand. Do your books accurately reflect your spending? Are either of you deceiving the other or are you both trying to ignore a potential money problem? Come clean. Admit to any deception. Set up safeguards that will keep you honest (e.g., a weekly financial review with your partner, a written budget). And begin again.

Talk about your emotional needs.

A big reason harmful residue accumulates in many marriages is the misconception that my partner should meet all my emotional needs. Whether it be feelings of sadness, rejection, anxiety, disappointment, worry, frustration, tension, or whatever, we often believe our spouse should soothe them. The truth is, however, that no human being can do this. And if you are expecting them to, you are doomed to disappointment.

The solution is twofold. First, talk to your spouse about your emotional needs. If you are feeling neglected, say so. If you are wanting to be admired, let him or her know. If you don't talk about your emotional needs, it can be nearly impossible for your spouse to meet them. And second, cultivate your relationship with God. Within each of us is a God-shaped void, an emptiness that can only be filled by God. And until we find our connection with God, we will always suffer twinges of disappointment in our marriage. Jesus has promised never to leave us or forsake us (see Matthew 28:20). He hears us when we pray.

Marriage is a place of great solace, but it cannot compare to the ultimate comfort that comes only through a relationship with God. So, face the fact that your partner can never meet all your needs, no matter how loving he or she is. Don't whine and complain about how he or she doesn't meet this need or that need. Instead, talk to your mate about your feelings and be sure to talk to God too. To get the two of you talking about your emotional needs, ask each other to identify an emotional deficit from the past month that needs more attention from your partner.

Talk about your anger.

One of the most toxic forms of marital residue is anger. And every marriage has more than enough of it. Anger rears its head when a spouse feels attacked or shortchanged. And for some quick-tempered spouses, anger becomes a chronic pattern of self-defeating rage whose trigger is unpredictable. When this is the case, when a person becomes a true rage-aholic, it's time for professional help. But even if you and your partner have managed to avoid this kind of hostility, you no doubt still struggle with anger.

Growing up, most of us don't get much practice with dealing with our anger. In fact, we're taught to fear such feelings. The truth is that anger is normal and natural. We are not responsible for being angry, only for how we respond to and use anger once it appears. The apostle Paul understood this when he said, "In your anger do not sin" (Ephesians 4:26).

So when it comes to ridding your marriage of harmful residue, you will want to give this emotion special attention. Understand that, while it comes part and parcel with most marriages, anger should not—by a long shot—be given free license. Anger requires limits and must be talked about routinely. The healthy handling of it begins with admitting you are (or were) angry. Most of us want to deny the presence of anger to control it. But that never works. Repressed anger has a high rate of resurrection. So 'fess up. Own your anger without hiding it or projecting it onto your partner.

Once you have admitted your anger, the next step is to release your vindictiveness—and this is not always easy. When we become angry, we feel that someone has hurt us, and we want to hurt them back. But we fool ourselves into believing that the only way to obtain satisfaction from being offended is to repay evil for evil. Once we become consumed by balancing the score, anger takes center stage in our marriage and is destined to do damage. So do your best to "turn the other cheek" (see Matthew 5:38–48). This practical principle releases revenge and is an insurance policy against resentment. How do you do this? By talking to your partner about how you feel hurt and then surrendering your desire to hurt him or her back. Let your partner know you are letting it go. And if you are inclined, say a prayer that God would protect you both from the reemergence of angry feelings.

Give each other freedom to fail.

"This morning we are going to learn to juggle. Each of you should be holding three brightly colored scarves." More than a thousand psychologists and physicians had gathered in the ballroom of the Disneyland Hotel for a conference on laughter. This morning we were listening to Dr. Steve Allen Jr., the son of the famous comedian.

"I'm going to lead you through a dozen steps to teach you the fine art of juggling," he told us. "First, take one of your scarves, hold it out at arm's length, and drop it."

We couldn't believe our ears. "Drop it?" people murmured. You could feel the resistance. Nobody around me dropped a scarf. And I certainly wasn't going to fall for that trick.

"C'mon now, drop it!" Dr. Allen commanded. One by one, we reluctantly released our scarves, and they fluttered to the carpeted ballroom floor.

"There now, doesn't that feel better?" asked Dr. Allen. "You have gotten your mistake over with. This is the first critical step in learning to juggle. We call it the guilt-free drop."

I could feel the tension roll off my shoulders. *I'm allowed to make mistakes,* I thought. *I don't have to be a perfect juggler.*

And you and I don't have to be perfect people to have a great marriage. We are all human. We all make mistakes.

Because of this very fact, we must give each other the freedom to fail. If you don't, you'll never rid yourselves of harmful residue. And when you are having difficulty letting go of a hurtful mistake by your partner, it is time to consider our next piece of advice on forgiveness.

Forgive when you feel hurt.

During a children's sermon one Sunday morning, Pastor Glenn E. Schaeffer held up an ugly-looking summer shirt that he wore occasionally around the house. He explained to the children that someone said the shirt was ugly and should be thrown away.

"This really hurt me," he explained. "I'm having trouble forgiving the person who said those mean things. Do you think I should forgive that person?" he asked the children.

Immediately, his six-year-old daughter, Alicia, raised her hand. "Yes, you should," she said without hesitation.

"But why? The person hurt my feelings," Schaeffer responded.

To which Alicia wisely answered, "Because you're married to her."

Out of the mouths of babes, right? We do need to forgive each other if for no other reason than because we *are* married. And no marriage, no matter how good, can survive without forgiveness. We are bound to get hurt. It's inevitable.

Here's a secret we learned about forgiveness from one of our friends and former professors, Lewis Smedes: Carrying rage and resentment against our partner does more harm to us than to them. That's why "the first and often the only person to be healed by forgiveness, is the person who does the forgiving," says Lew in *Forgive and Forget*. "When we genuinely forgive, we set a prisoner free and then discover that the prisoner we set free was us."

In a healthy marriage, two people help one another become better at forgiving by asking for forgiveness, as well as by giving it when needed. "I'm sorry. Will you forgive me?" These simple words offer a possible way out of the inevitable blame game that traps so many couples—and they are sure to release you from the harmful residue that would otherwise bog you down.

Protect each other from hurry sickness.

This step is preventive in nature. It will help you keep harmful residue to a minimum in the months to come. Why? Because when you or your partner are constantly overextended, always reacting to crises, continually trying to tie up loose ends, you are increasing the potential for problems between you. It's a fact. The more hassled and frazzled you feel, the more you will bicker and fight.

So in an attempt to keep harmful residue at a minimum next month, talk about what you can do together to slow down your pace. Would doing some planning on meal preparation help? Maybe filling up the gas tank before it gets too near empty. How about coordinating your schedules for the next month right now so you minimize the surprises? Perhaps it would help to create a system for organizing your receipts so you don't have a frantic search for records when it comes time to balance the books. And what about taxiing the kids from place to place? The more planning you do now, as you are ridding yourselves of harmful residue, the less residue you will have to contend with next month.

Update how well you know your spouse.

Mrs. Albert Einstein was once asked if she understood her husband's theory of relativity. "No," she said, "but I know how he likes his tea."

Good answer. Knowing simple intimacies about your partner is at the heart of a healthy marriage. And keeping up-to-date on those ever-changing intimacies is a healthy habit loving couples cannot ignore. So in your pursuit to rid yourselves of harmful residue, take a moment to check in with your spouse. What would he or she like you to know? Maybe your wife wants you to know she's feeling especially vulnerable about her mother's health and needs you to be sensitive about the mounting phone bill because of the calls she's going to be making this month. Maybe your husband is feeling especially anxious about a project at work this month and needs you to know he may be coming home a little later than usual over the next couple weeks.

A quick update will keep next month's harmful residue to a minimum. If you know your phone bill may be higher because of your mother-in-law's health, it's less likely to be a problem. Same is true if you know to expect your husband home a little late because of a stressful situation at work. A little warning can go a long way in minimizing harmful residue from accumulating for next month. To get you started on this topic, ask each other: What do I need to know about you that I may not know already?

For Reflection

1. Is there any unfinished business you and your partner need to talk about?

2. Have you felt lonely lately? How can your partner help you feel less alone, less isolated in certain areas of your life?

3. Is there a money issue you and your partner need to discuss? Are you being honest with each other when it comes to your spending habits?

4. Have you been angry with your partner this month? If so, explore with him or her what's going on and why you sometimes feel this way.

5. How can you better support one another emotionally or practically in the next four weeks? Be specific.

6. To keep your marriage current, ask each other what has defined you in the past month. What has been on your mind the most?

Once a Month . . .

FIRE UP PASSION IN THE BEDROOM

> *Thrills come at the beginning and do not last. . . . Let the thrill go and you will find you are living in a world of new thrills.*
>
> C. S. LEWIS

Sarah was in grade school when she heard a number of new words at school from other students. She asked her mother about them. Her mom said, "Sarah, those are words that people use to crudely describe something God gave us to enjoy." Like a pro, her mom went on to explain the facts of life.

Puzzled and shocked, Sarah, one of three children, asked her mom, "You mean you and Daddy did that three times?"

You may be wondering if we have a similar mindset because we are placing this healthy habit of firing up passion in the bedroom in the category of "once a month." Even before we wrote this chapter our editor was ribbing us: "Only once a month?" Not exactly. We're not saying you should only make love with your spouse once a month. We have something else in mind, and it will shed plenty of light on quality as well as quantity.

In fact, a landmark study of over seven thousand married people found that the frequency of marital sex was strongly associated with how couples rate their sexual satisfaction. Nine out of ten of the couples who were having sex three or more times a week reported satisfaction with the quality of their sex lives. In contrast, only half of those individuals who were having sex once a month were satisfied. All that to say, this healthy habit is not about limiting your sexual encounters with each other to once every thirty days. Quite the opposite.

What Firing Up Passion in the Bedroom Can Do for Your Marriage

We were speaking at a large marriage conference not long ago, and after one of our sessions we slid into a workshop whose topic caught our eye: "How to Have Kids and a Sex Life, Too." Workshop leaders Pam and Rich Batten warmed up the group by asking couples which movie title best described their sex life: *The Fast and the Furious, Dr. Doolittle,* or *The Mummy Returns.* There wasn't a show of hands, but *Dr. Doolittle* got the most chuckles.

In the discussion that followed, couples were quick to rattle off obstacles to a satisfactory love life: no energy, no privacy, no spontaneity, kids banging on doors, and so on. Each complaint engendered nods and groans of agreement. It seems nearly every couple, married long enough, understands the struggle to keep their sex life filled with passion. What most couples don't understand is how an intentional effort—once every thirty days—can keep the flames of passion burning on all the others.

Let's make this clear. Sex is critically important for a quality marriage. We'll say it again. Sex makes a significant impact on whether you will rate your marriage as satisfying or not.

In one survey on the importance of sex for marriage, the results were compelling: Couples who rated their sex lives positively also rated their marriages positively, and those who rated their sex lives negatively rated their marriages negatively as well. In other words, if couples report that sex is unimportant to them, it is very likely that they view their entire marriage as unhappy. Both the quantity and quality of sex in marriage are central to a good overall relationship.

You might be relieved to know that a number of factors other than frequency of sexual interaction have also been linked to satisfaction with marital sex. Mutuality in initiating sex can be an important contributor to sexual satisfaction of both wives and husbands. It also appears that women who take an active role during sexual sharing are more likely to be pleased with their sex lives than those who assume a more passive role.

No study states that a high-quality sex life is an absolute requirement for a high-quality marriage, nor that a good sex life guarantees a good marriage. Nonetheless, studies consistently suggest that quality of sex and quality of marriage do go together in most cases. For this reason, the healthy habit of firing up passion is critical.

How to Fire Up Passion in the Bedroom

Contrary to popular opinion, a married couple's sex life does not have to dissipate. If you are intentional, marriage provides the greatest sex possible. It's a gift neither singles nor cohabiting couples enjoy. Consider this: Married people are about twice as likely as unmarried people to make love at least two or three times a week. And that's not all: Married sex is more fun. Forty-eight percent of husbands say sex with their

Assessing Your Passion Quotient

So how's your love life? Do you enjoy sex as often as you'd like? And when you do have sex, is it satisfying? The following self-test will help you answer these questions. So take a moment, individually, to answer these questions as honestly as you can, then compare your answers with each other.

T   F   I would rate our sex life as good.

T   F   My spouse would rate our sex life as good.

T   F   We sometimes deliberately schedule our times of sexual play together.

T   F   I know specific ways to please my partner and make him or her feel sexually satisfied.

T   F   We have productive talks with each other about our sex life and how to make it better.

T   F   I'm happy with both the frequency and the quality of our sexual times together.

T   F   If I were to take a test on sexuality for married adults, I'd get an A.

T   F   We both know the date of our next planned sexual experience together.

T   F   We make at least one monthly purchase (e.g., lingerie, scented lotion) that helps us spice up our sex life.

T   F   We have specific times when we eagerly anticipate being together for passion and intimacy.

Add up the number of "true" responses. If it is eight or higher, you're doing pretty well with your sex life. Count your blessings. If your score isn't that high, however, you are like a lot of other couples and can benefit from the tips we offer in this chapter for firing up passion.

partners is extremely satisfying, compared to just thirty-seven percent of cohabiting men. When it comes to creating a lasting sexual union, marriage implies at least a promise of permanence, which may be why cohabiting men are four times more likely to cheat, and cohabiting women eight times more likely, than husbands and wives, according to Linda J. Waite and Maggie Gallagher in *The Case for Marriage.*

As a married couple you have the opportunity to make your love life better than you ever imagined by cultivating this healthy habit. We'll warn you that it requires intentional work, but the dividends are invaluable for loving couples. Here's how.

Talk to each other about sex or ask for what you'd like.

We'll start with the bottom line in getting your sexual needs met: Assume that your partner doesn't know how to satisfy you. It doesn't matter how long you've been married, beginning with this premise will help you set the stage for developing the habit of asking for what you'd like. That's the key and research bears it out. In one survey, eighty-eight percent of the women who reported always discussing their sexual feelings with their spouses described their sex lives as good or very good. In contrast, only thirty percent of the women who reported never discussing sex with their partners described their sex lives as good or very good.

What makes each of you happy is not necessarily the same thing. Your needs, in fact, may be dramatically different. So do not make the mistake of assuming your partner knows how to meet your sexual needs if you do not talk to each other about it. This is rule number one for firing up passion in the bedroom.

Schedule a sex date.

This sounds so cold. So unromantic. But make no mistake, a fulfilling sex life for almost every busy couple depends on it. So here goes: Get your date books ready and at least once a month, schedule a specific time when the two of you can enjoy a leisurely time of passionate sex. We know this sounds artificial. We can hear you groaning right now. But please do not make the mistake of thinking this advice is for other couples. Every busy couple can benefit from this. You can obviously have spontaneous sex anytime you are so inclined, but this once-a-month "meeting" is key to firing up passion in the bedroom. The next few points will show you how it works.

Guard your time fiercely.

Once you agree on a time that will work—a time when you are not distracted by kids or projects, and a time when you are not exhausted—protect it. This time is specifically set aside for the two of you. Don't allow something "urgent" to steal it away. Let's face it, a dozen potential things could interfere with your schedules. But hold to this time, knowing that your marriage is going to be better for it. Besides that, it's going to be a lot of fun.

Have a plan.

If you are meeting at home over a long lunch hour or on a weekend when the kids are at Grandma's, be sure you think through what will make this time the best it can be for each of you. Do you want music? A clean house? Silk sheets on the bed? A time to shower beforehand? A bath together? Candles? What would be your ideal of how to make this time everything you want it to be? Talk it through. Don't make your spouse guess what you like; say what's on your mind.

And go shopping. In the weeks preceding your time together, be on the lookout for lingerie and such that will make this time special. Before we got married, somebody gave me (Les) a copy of Charlie Shedd's book, *Letters to Phillip*, and in it he suggested that a husband should never skimp on the lingerie budget. Pretty good advice. You don't have to break the bank, but for these once-a-month occasions, it's a good idea to splurge a little.

Enjoy the anticipation.

Part of what makes this once-a-month experience so beneficial to couples is the anticipation. Just knowing that you will have this dedicated time to enjoy each other to the fullest will make it all the more special. So give in to the anticipation. Say things to each other like, "Only two more weeks," "I can't wait for the eighteenth," or, "Have you been thinking about our time as much as I have?"

Another way to heighten the anticipation is to send a card or note to your partner. Leave him or her a voice mail at work. You may even want to send something romantic that your partner could wear when you have your time together. The point is to conjure up expectancy and eagerness. Don't allow your appointment to simply roll around on the calendar like any ordinary meeting. Give it special attention, and let the excitement mount.

Overcome sexual ignorance.

The more you know the more you enjoy. It's that simple. In today's sex-saturated environment, it is difficult to imagine that we need sex education as married adults, but we do. And attending a seminar or reading a self-help book on the subject is an ideal way to improve your education. Our good friends, Cliff and Joyce Penner, are two of the most knowledgeable people we know on the subject of sex. By the way, any one of their numerous books on sex would be a great resource along these lines (for example, *The Gift of Sex* or *Restoring the Pleasure*). Some time ago, when the four of us were out to dinner, Cliff and Joyce told us about the letters and e-mails they receive after conducting their seminar "Enjoying the Gift of Sex." The sexual breakthroughs couples have as a result of acquiring accurate sexual knowledge at their seminars was simply outstanding. Countless couples write to them to express appreciation for everything from teaching them new techniques to exposing sexual myths, and for filling in the gaps in their knowledge.

We can't come close to giving you all the information you need in this little chapter. There may be a missing link in your sexual knowledge that could revolutionize your sex life, and there is no way for us to know what it might be. So we encourage you, as a couple, to attend a good seminar or study a good book on the subject, and push back your level of sexual ignorance.

What men need to know about women.

Here's a little review from Female Sexuality 101. Maybe you don't need it, but most men do. Women, unlike men, do not separate sex from the relational and emotional aspects of the relationship. They want a sense of connection for more than an hour before sex is initiated. They want an overarching atmosphere of intimacy and affection built on daily choices. As Kevin Leman says it, "Sex begins in the kitchen." For this reason, it is critically important to communicate in loving ways throughout the day and give your wife special attention. For women, sex has much more to it than physical arousal.

Your wife is also more vulnerable to distraction when it comes to sex. If she is fatigued, feeling hurt, or struggling with her body image, she may have difficulty focusing on her sexual drive. So do your best to minimize distractions by paying attention to what dampens her sexual desires.

After a man has had an orgasm, he requires some recuperative time. Women, on the other hand, can have a series of orgasms, one right after the other (as many as five or more separate orgasms in a couple of minutes). Some men, wanting to be "the world's greatest lover," get hung up on keeping track of their wife's orgasms. That's the wrong approach. It is better to focus on helping your wife enjoy the sexual experience, and to let go of keeping score.

What women need to know about men.

Men, unlike women, often view making love as a primary way of connecting with their mates. In other words, their sexual activity can stem from an inability to connect in other ways, like conversations and nonsexual touching. For this reason your husband's sex drive may be more apparent than yours. If so, enjoy it as you allow yourselves to tap into your sexual desire.

Men are geared more than women for immediate gratification. If he sees you getting ready for a party and it turns him on, he probably won't be satisfied with a long kiss and a few caresses. You may be thinking about being late to the party or messing up your lipstick, but he loves the excitement of the moment, even if brief. This may not be your idea of an ideal sexual encounter, but sometimes accommodating his quickness is a loving gift that he will appreciate as much as you enjoy the more leisurely approach.

You have undoubtedly noticed that your husband is prone to visual stimulation. It serves as a sexual cue to him. For example, you may seldom notice your husband getting out of the shower, but he notices you. He can become aroused by catching a quick glimpse of you on an exercise machine or even doing something as mundane as a simple chore. It often takes very little for your husband to become aroused because he is more visually oriented than you. So be ready for the unexpected, and relish his attraction toward you.

For Reflection

1. If you are feeling creative, give a movie title to your sex life for the past thirty days. If your creativity is waning, simply describe your sex life for the last month to each other.

2. If you could change one thing about your recent sex life, what would it be?

3. Be honest with each other about how you would feel to schedule a deliberate intimate night together in bed. What do you like and dislike about this? What do you fear about doing this?

4. Discuss in specific terms when you could schedule a special night together this month.

5. Explore with each other what would make this time especially gratifying or meaningful to each of you. Is there something specific you would like your partner to wear or do?

Once a Year . . .

> Chains do not hold a marriage together.
> It is threads, hundreds of tiny threads which sew
> people together through the years.
>
> SIMONE SIGNORET

Once a Year . . .

REVIEW YOUR TOP-TEN HIGHLIGHTS

> *History is a hill or high point of vantage, from which alone men see the town in which they live or the age in which they are living.*
>
> G. K. CHESTERTON

When we got married in 1984, just out of college, Les gave me an irreplaceable gift. Without me knowing, Les had saved every ticket stub and every little memento from every date we had ever been on and organized them in a book where he recorded a few thoughts and recollections of each one. I couldn't believe it. From our first date at a Kansas City Royals game, to an art museum, to the zoo, to concerts. They were all there. He didn't miss one. Needless to say, I was impressed. Not just that he would do this but that he would do it for so long. You see, we dated for seven years before we got married. No joke. For seven years, Les collected and reflected all on his own and then presented me with three volumes of priceless memories.

I can't count how many times we have gone through the pages of these books and recalled details of dates that would have been lost forever if he hadn't taken the time to preserve them. Truthfully, I don't know which has been more fun: the dates themselves, or the time we have spent remembering them. Each page of this treasure evokes specific feelings and memories. And each time we review them we join our spirits together.

I'd give a lot of money to have seminar volumes for each year of our married life. Apparently, Les's romantic ways reached a limit—like they do for most men—once we crossed the proverbial marital threshold. It wasn't that we quit having fun—not at all. It's just that neither he nor I kept any record . . . until more recently.

A few years back, Les started a journal that now rivals the three-volume dating books. And on the eve of most New Year celebrations, we steal away and review the past 365 days to come up with a list of our top-ten highlights of the year.

Celebrating our fifteenth wedding anniversary at Sno-qualmi Lodge made the list. So did a cookout on the Oregon coast with Kevin and Kathy. Les's achieving his promotion to full professor at the university made the list too. As did brunch at the Four Seasons Hotel in New York City and a sunny walk around Central Park with friends. The thrill of finding out we had a baby on the way certainly made the list, as well.

We've been making a list of the top-ten highlights of our years together since 1997. I suppose we've always reminisced about our times together, but not until '97 did we begin to take it seriously and actually review our year and write down our highlights. Now, with several years of this under our belt, we've got to say these lists are a true treasure to us. They are a record of our positive recollections that we wouldn't trade for anything.

Maybe you do the same thing. But if you don't, it's time to consider cultivating this annual habit. It's sure to give your marriage wings. It's sure to bring you to a vantage point where you will breathe deep and take in a sweeping view of all that's blessed your lives together.

Why Reviewing Your Top-Ten Highlights Is Important

"We made it through another year." Ever heard somebody say this? Have you uttered this sentence yourself? For too many of us, our initial thoughts about the past are negative. An invisible magnet draws us to recall instances where we wish something would have been different. *If only we'd made more money. If only the weather had cooperated. If only I had not gotten sick this past winter.* "If only." It's the mantra of too many good people, and it's contaminating their marriages.

The healthy habit of reviewing your highlights will steer you clear from unproductive thinking like this and set you on a positive path that's sure to reward you with more blessings. This habit also sets you up for succeeding in the annual ritual we describe in the next chapter—charting your course for the coming year. It's next to impossible for most of us to get energized about being proactive with our future if we don't take time to reflect on what we've enjoyed in our past. So this exercise serves as a kind of fuel to propel us forward and increase the likelihood of more success and happiness. And that's reason enough to annually review your highlights.

How to Review Your Top-Ten Highlights

For some, just hearing about this habit is enough to get them started doing it. For others, a few tips and pointers can

Assessing How Well You Review

So how are you doing when it comes to recalling your yearly high points? Have you cut a groove into your marriage that makes this an annual habit? The following self-test will help you answer these questions. So take a moment, individually, to answer these questions as honestly as you can, then compare your answers with each other.

T F We have an annual system already in place for recalling our happiest memories.

T F We have several photo albums that cover the years of our marriage.

T F We often reminisce about good times we've shared together.

T F I feel routinely energized by recalling times we have enjoyed.

T F I can tell you what outstanding events uniquely marked each of the last three years of our marriage.

T F I can think of something new and specific we enjoyed this past year that will inspire us to repeat it this year.

T F We take lots of photographs through the year.

T F One or both of us keeps a journal or diary of some kind.

T F We've laughed at some point during the last month about an experience we had together long ago.

T F We take videos of special occasions.

Add up the number of "true" responses. If it is eight or higher, you can rest assured that you are doing an excellent job of reviewing your highlights. If your score isn't that high, however, you have a bit of work to do and will certainly benefit from the tips we offer in this chapter for remembering and celebrating your life together.

go a long way. So with this in mind, we offer a few ideas that will help you bring this ritual into your own marriage.

Keep some kind of easy record.

Every year I (Les) have students in my courses who don't take notes. "Dr. Parrott, I'm a visual learner," they tell me. "I don't need to take notes." I never know what to say to these students. Typically their grade on the final exam says it all. The point being that it is very difficult for us humans to retain information if we do not rely on a few memory joggers.

This is true even when it comes to recalling positive experiences we have enjoyed through a year. At the time, we think we'll never forget the joy of seeing our child play soccer, how relaxing it was to watch the sunset on the pier, or how utterly happy we were just to share a quiet meal together at a new restaurant where the food and service made for a perfect evening. But the chances of not recalling many of these times is significant if we don't keep track of them.

Now, this little task may require discipline—perhaps more than any of the other habits noted in this book. And not everyone likes to keep records. That's understood. But if you want to enjoy the benefits of this annual habit, you've got to find a way to keep a record of what you've enjoyed together. For us, that means relying on Les's journal where he simply writes a sentence each day of what happened. For you it may be more elaborate. Or maybe you could reconstruct your year from an orderly photo album. Or maybe you are not orderly at all, and you both enjoy the challenge of piecing together your year. Whatever your style, this habit begins with keeping a record.

Decide what constitutes a highlight.

When you hear the word *highlight*, what comes to mind? Does it involve travel? An expensive meal? A holiday? Special gifts? Well, it certainly can involve any of these fine things, but we don't want you to limit yourself to them. Look beyond extravagance to include simple highlights. A wonderful day of working in your garden together. A road trip. Redecorating your living room. Opening your home to kids traveling through on a church choir tour. Playing flag football with friends. Making a tasty meal together in your kitchen. Attending your child's first Little League game. Volunteering in a soup kitchen downtown. These kinds of experiences are not costly, but they may just be one of your top-ten moments together over the last twelve months.

Highlights come in all shapes and sizes. They are simply points in time where the wave crests. High points are moments when the two of you enjoy life the way God intended it. They are little glimpses of heaven on earth. So, sure, your two weeks in Maui at a luxury resort certainly qualify, but don't restrict yourself to thinking true highlights cost money.

Make the review a memorable tradition.

Once you have what you need to begin your review, choose a time and a place that will make it memorable. Of course, there are dozens of options. You may want to begin this tradition on your anniversary, for example. Or maybe you want to do this at some point during the Thanksgiving holiday, as you thank God for your blessings. Or maybe, like us, you'll choose to do this around New Year's.

For the past several years we've taken time during New Year's to sit down with Les's journal and simply read through it. Somewhere along the line Chinese food factored into this experience, and ordering Chinese takeout has become a part of our tradition. We eat and talk and make our list. In fact, we write our list in the back of the ten-year journal we keep, where it resides next to the previous years' lists, handy for a quick review at any point throughout the year.

Use photos and video if you can.

We know some couples who have incorporated this yearly exercise into their marriage with a multimedia presentation, or at least by having a night of organizing their year's photo album. One couple we know has an elegant album with the year embossed on the spine. Their series of albums stand prominently in a row on their living room bookshelf. Still other couples review their year with video footage. Of course, this requires a special interest and hobby, but if it works for you, great!

Enjoy the process.

"Hurry up and get in here so we can review our year; I've got to clean the house and get the kids to bed." If you hear yourself saying something along these lines, put this exercise on hold. You're not in a place to reap the rewards of an annual review of your highlights. Instead, schedule a baby-sitter, set aside the time this deserves, and enjoy the experience of it with your spouse. The point of this annual habit is not to check it off your to-do list and move on to your next task. This is an occasion to savor. So take your time and enjoy the process.

For Reflection

1. When you think about starting this little tradition of reviewing your year, what kinds of feelings does it conjure up? What do you like and dislike about it?

2. Is there a specific time that would work best for the two of you to do this? No need to focus only on January 1 of each year. Maybe your anniversary or another date would work best. What do you think?

3. How would you like to go about preserving your memories together? Journal? Photos? Video? Who will be responsible for collecting and organizing the results, or will you share that task?

4. What will constitute a highlight for the two of you to record?

5. How would you like to celebrate your highlights? Does your style lend itself to an informal family night looking at photos or a yearly dinner or dessert that is just for the two of you?

Once a Year . . .

CHART YOUR COURSE
FOR THE COMING YEAR

> *Love does not consist in gazing at each other but in looking together in the same direction.*
>
> ANTOINE DE SAINT-EXUPÉRY

You're driving to a new location when she begins wondering whether you are going in the right direction.

"Does this seem right to you?" she asks.

"I'm not sure," you reply, "but let's see what's up the road a bit."

"Why don't we ask directions?" she asks.

That's when you know you have arrived at one of the prototypical marriage moments that defines all couples. And that's when you drive faster, right? "I know where I'm going," you will say, as if you've suddenly tuned into an internal navigational system that only you can read.

You both know the experience. We've all lived it. And more than likely we will repeat it many times. But when it comes to setting out on the metaphorical journey of marriage each year, we can't afford to wander without a true and clear sense of direction. So we dedicate this final chapter—this final healthy habit—to helping you find your way as you chart your course for the coming year.

What does it mean to chart your course? It means being proactive about where you'd like to be as a couple twelve months from now. Rather than moving through life simply reacting to outside forces, it means taking charge and sitting in the driver's seat. Far too many couples ride like passengers on a bumpy bus, watching the scenery flash by their window as life passes by.

We'll be honest. Setting your course for the coming year is not easy. It requires hard work and initiative. It will ask that you take responsibility for the condition of your marriage. It will then demand that you make the sacrifices to make your dreams a reality. In other words, the kind of marriage you want will be forged from your efforts. Make no mistake, you will never achieve your ideal marriage as a mere passenger; you and your partner must have your hands on the wheel. In his play *Don Juan in Hell*, George Bernard Shaw correctly concluded: "Hell is to drift, heaven is to steer." This chapter will show you how to steer your marriage in the direction of heaven on earth.

What Charting Your Course Will Do for Your Marriage

Charting the course of your marriage raises the quality of life for you and your family and keeps you from the "Someday Syndrome." Think about it. That single word—*someday*—denotes idle thinking rarely backed by action. And most well-intentioned people regularly utter it. But the smart couple moves beyond daydreams by charting their course for a reality where dreams come true.

Motivational speaker and writer Zig Ziglar tells of a man who went next door to borrow his neighbor's lawnmower. The neighbor explained that the man could not use the mower because all the flights had been canceled from New York to Los Angeles. The would-be borrower asked him what canceled flights from New York to Los Angeles had to do with borrowing the lawnmower.

"It doesn't have anything to do with it," the neighbor replied. "But if I don't want to let you use my lawnmower, one excuse is as good as another."

Some couples go though life day after day, year after year, piling one excuse on top of another for the state of their marriage. They look for any reason to avoid charting their course and blame it on fate, in-laws, lack of money, their temperament, the government, or even their church. Charting your course does away with the blame game and puts an end to excuses. It gives you the opportunity to make your marriage everything you want it to be.

How to Chart Your Course for the Coming Year

A friend of ours took his seven-year-old son on a sight-seeing tour of Washington, D.C. They explored the Capitol, the Lincoln Memorial, and the Air and Space Museum. When they got to the Washington Monument, the missile-minded youngster stared and said, "They'll never get it off the ground."

Some couples feel the same way about charting the course of their marriage. The weight of trying to figure out your direction can feel daunting. So in this chapter we offer you some of the best advice we have for making this potentially weighty endeavor doable.

Assessing How Well You Chart Your Course

So how are you doing when it comes to charting your course as a couple? Do you feel you both have a strong sense of direction and purpose? The following self-test will help you answer these questions. So take a moment, individually, to answer these questions as honestly as you can, then compare your answers with each other.

T F   We've discussed our goals as a couple for this coming year.

T F   We have written our goals down and keep them in a visible place as a reminder.

T F   Most people getting a behind-the-scenes look at our marriage would say we are deliberate about where we are headed as a couple.

T F   We often pray that God will guide our steps and all our decisions as husband and wife.

T F   We have a mission statement we have written for our marriage.

T F   I have something specific I'd like to change about our marriage.

T F   We have set our priorities and know what matters most to us in our marriage.

T F   Both of us are positive people who steer clear of pessimism.

T F   We make resolutions together.

T F   We consciously work at trusting God with our future, knowing that ultimately it is out of our hands.

Add up the number of "true" responses. If it is eight or higher, you can rest assured that you are doing an excellent job of charting your course for the coming year. If your score isn't that high, however, you have a bit of work to do and will certainly benefit from the tips we offer in this chapter.

Ask for divine guidance.

In December 1995 American Airlines Flight 965 departed from Miami on a regularly scheduled trip to Cali, Columbia. On the landing approach, the pilot of the 757 needed to select the next radio navigation fix, named Rozo. He entered an R into his navigation computer. The computer returned a list of nearby navigation fixes starting with R, and the pilot selected the first of these, whose latitude and longitude appeared to be correct. Unfortunately, instead of Rozo, the pilot selected Romeo, 132 miles to the northeast. Following indications on the flight computer, the pilots began an easterly turn and slammed into a granite peak at ten thousand feet. More than 150 people aboard perished.

The plane navigated the same way all modern jumbo jets do. When the plane is on course, the needle on the control panel is centered, but the needle gives no indication whatsoever about the correctness of the selected radio beacon. The gauge looks pretty much the same just before landing as it does just before crashing. The computer told the pilot he was tracking precisely to the beacon he had selected. Unfortunately, it neglected to tell him the beacon he selected was a fatal choice.

In much the same sense we can set the direction for our marriage without knowing whether it is the best direction for us. So as you chart your course for this coming year, bathe the process in prayer, and ask God to guide you. This is the first and most important step of this annual exercise.

Consider what matters most.

In the aftermath of the horrific tragedy that struck our nation on September 11, 2001, we were deeply touched by some of the notes and letters we received from couples around the country. They wrote to tell us how this act of terrorism impacted their marriages. More specifically, they told us how hearing some of the conversations between couples—when they knew they would never speak again—moved them.

"When I heard the cell phone calls made by loved ones soon before their deaths," wrote one man, "I thought about what I would say to my wife if I were to call her in the seconds before I die. I recognized that I could not possibly tell her all the beauty she has brought to my life, and what an incredible person she is to me—not in those few moments, not on short notice." He went on to tell us that he took the time to tell his wife what mattered most to him, on his own schedule, "not on death's timetable."

This is an opportunity we all have. And as you chart your course for your coming year of marriage, we urge you to do this too. Take some time to inventory what really matters most to both of you in your relationship. What are the things you prize about what you have built together? And what do you prize about your partner? Maybe it's the way you lift one another up in tough times. Maybe it's your shared sense of humor. Perhaps one of the things you value most in your marriage is how you bring one another closer to God. Or how your spouse hones your personal vision and gives you confidence. Whatever it is, make a list of what matters most. This will set you up for our next tip.

Write a mission statement, and revisit it yearly.

If you are serious about charting the course of your marriage, you will need a statement of purpose. Once you take inventory of what matters most, your mission statement will serve as your compass.

Begin with the words "Our purpose is . . ." Take a stab at it. There is no precise way to do this. Simply draft some ideas and don't get hung up on making this the perfect and ultimate statement. Some of the most advanced corporations make a practice of revisiting their mission statement every so often. They study the document that sets forth their original aims and then measure their performance. At regular intervals companies look at whether the aims of the business have fallen out of sync with its mission statement, whether these aims need to be brought back into line, or whether the statement itself needs to be rewritten to reflect current realities. As couples, we need to do the same thing. A purpose statement keeps our marriage on track.

"Intimate relationships cannot substitute for a life plan," said Harriet Lerner. "But to have any meaning or viability at all, a life plan must include intimate relationships." We couldn't agree more. That's why we urge you to write a mission statement for your marriage.

Consider what you'd like to change.

If you could press a magic button, what would you change in your marriage? Perhaps you'd like to enjoy more romance. Maybe you'd like to have fewer quarrels. Would you prefer to have more meals as a family with the television off? Every couple has things they'd like to change. Make a list of no more than a half dozen things you wish were different. Why? Because this will serve as the springboard for setting goals that will help you improve your relationship over the next twelve months. After all, if you could do something that would increase your marital satisfaction by ten percent, wouldn't you do it? Of course. And that's exactly what setting goals will help you do.

Set specific goals.

Just as your marriage mission statement serves as your compass, your goals will serve as your road map directing you, step by step, toward achieving your purpose. What goals would you like to achieve in your marriage this next year? Put your goals in writing and make them visible. You know the drill. You've written goals down before. But know this, all the goals in the world mean nothing if a person does not have the stick-to-it attitude to make them materialize.

In his compelling book *Me: The Narcissistic American*, psychoanalyst Aaron Stern gets right to the point: "To attain emotional maturity, each of us must learn to develop . . . the ability to delay immediate gratification in favor of long-range goals." That's the key. Delayed gratification. And the beauty of this sometimes elusive quality of character is that it becomes more abundant in marriage—as we will show you in the next tip.

Understand the power of making resolutions together.

"Every New Year, I resolve to streamline my body, be more sensitive to others, and be more productive. And every year, my resolutions fail." We hear something to this effect from dozens of people in our counseling office about the time March rolls around each year. If you've set resolutions for yourself before, you probably know the feeling. In fact, only twenty-two percent of respondents to a *Newsweek* poll believed they would actually stand by their resolutions for a complete year. Well, here's some good news: Couples who make resolutions together for the good of their marriage are far more likely to make their resolutions last than those making resolutions on their own.

"Teamwork wins goals," notes Terry D. Hargrave, a professor of marriage and family therapy at West Texas A and M University. "If a resolution is as good for your spouse as it is for you—bet on success with the resolution and a sweeter marriage." Why? Because you have a built-in support system for making the same resolutions work. You each have a cheerleader in each other.

Awaken your can-do attitude.

According to the United States Bureau of Standards, a dense fog covering seven city blocks to a depth of a hundred feet contains less liquid than one glass of water. That's important to remember because sometimes the littlest of irritants in a marriage can force one or both partners into a negative attitude that keeps them from reaching their goals. At times we let a small problem fog up our entire visual field. One little incident, such as a negative remark by your partner, can ruin your outlook. Take safeguards against this by keeping an upbeat attitude as you are charting your course. Don't say things like, "You could never do that," or, "We'll be having this same old discussion next year." If you do, you're probably right.

Trust God.

Brennan Manning, in his book *Ruthless Trust*, tells a poignant story that may help you remember this important point. When the brilliant ethicist John Kavanaugh went to work for three months at "the house of the dying" in Calcutta, he was seeking a clear answer as to how best to spend the rest of his life. On the first morning there he met Mother Teresa. She asked what she could do for him. When Kavanaugh asked her to pray for him, she asked what she could pray for. He said: "Pray that I have clarity."

She said firmly, "No, I will not do that." When he asked her why, she said, "Clarity is the last thing you are clinging to and must let go of." When Kavanaugh commented that she always seemed to have the clarity he longed for, she laughed and said, "I have never had clarity; what I have always had is trust. So I will pray that you trust God."

And we will pray the same for you, our readers. That as you chart your course for the coming year together as a couple, you will trust God to keep your marriage on track.

For Reflection

1. If you could make your marriage ten percent better in one specific area over the next twelve months, what would it be?

2. Do the two of you have a marital mission statement? If not, what might it look like? What would you want to be sure is in it?

3. How do you rate yourself, personally, as a goal setter? Talk with each other about your feelings when it comes to setting goals—individually and as a couple.

4. Explore ways to keep one another accountable with your goals. Could you set up "mile markers" (times to check in with each other on how you are doing) for this next year, and if so, when would they be?

5. Consider the following areas where you might want to set goals as a couple: spiritual goals, social goals, family goals, personal goals, financial goals, career goals, and recreational goals.

Conclusion:

PUTTING IT INTO PRACTICE

> *The problem in my life and other people's lives is not the absence of knowing what to do, but the absence of doing it.*
>
> PETER DRUCKER

There you have it—the ultimate to-do list for married couples—two things to do once a day, once a week, once a month, and once a year. Are you ready to put the list into practice? We hope so. Everyone knows a to-do list is only as good as the action it invokes. So we leave you with three simple suggestions.

First of all, keep the big picture in mind. Don't get hung up on the details of the Love List. Looking through a peephole is no way to stay motivated when you're moving toward a goal. The big view is important. It takes big dreams, big goals, big rewards, big faith, to keep us moving through obstacles and fatigue and discouragement. So maintain your marriage momentum by reminding yourselves what you are working toward. The goal is not to check things off your list. The goal is to build a better marriage.

Second, keep the Love List handy. You may even want to copy it in your own handwriting and place it on a card in your date book or somewhere you can look at it often. Putting the list on paper alerts the part of your brain known as the reticular activating system (the RAS). And the RAS evaluates whatever you tell it is essential or nonessential. As you cultivate the habits on the Love List, this part of your brain will be on the lookout for helping you spot opportunities to boost your partner's self-esteem, fire up passion in the bedroom, and all the rest. But you've got to keep it handy and read it often for this to happen. You may want to use the convenient adhesive copies of the Love List that came with this book to attach to the mirror where you get ready in the morning, or you may want to photocopy the Table of Contents and post it near your desk.

Our third suggestion is simple. Start now. English sociologist Arnold Toynbee put it well when he said, "The right moment for starting on your next job is not tomorrow or next week; it is *instanter*, or in the American idiom, 'right now.'"

So what are you waiting for? Start today by . . . taking time to touch and . . . finding something that makes you both laugh.

FOCUS ON THE FAMILY®

Welcome to the *Family*!

Whether you received this book as a gift, borrowed it from
a friend, or purchased it yourself, we're glad you read it! It's just
one of the many helpful, insightful, and encouraging
resources produced by Focus on the Family.

In fact, that's what Focus on the Family is all about—providing inspiration,
information, and biblically based advice to people in all stages of life.

It began in 1977 with the vision of one man, Dr. James Dobson, a licensed
psychologist and author of 16 best-selling books on marriage, parenting,
and family. Alarmed by the societal, political, and economic pressures
that were threatening the existence of the American family, Dr. Dobson
founded Focus on the Family with one employee—an assistant—
and a once-a-week radio broadcast, aired on only 36 stations.

Now an international organization, Focus on the Family is dedicated
to preserving Judeo-Christian values and strengthening the family
through more than 80 different ministries, including eight separate
daily radio broadcasts; television public service announcements;
10 publications; and a steady series of books and award-winning
films and videos for people of all ages and interests.

Recognizing the needs of—as well as the sacrifices and important
contributions made by—such diverse groups as educators, physicians,
attorneys, crisis pregnancy center staff, and single parents,
Focus on the Family offers specific outreaches to uphold and
minister to these individuals too. And it's all done for one purpose,
and one purpose only: to encourage and strengthen individuals
and families through the life-changing message of Jesus Christ.

•   •   •

For more information about the ministry, or if we can be of help to your
family, simply write to Focus on the Family, Colorado Springs, CO 80995
or call 1-800-A-FAMILY (1-800-232-6459). Friends in Canada may write
Focus on the Family, P.O. Box 9800, Stn. Terminal, Vancouver, B.C. V6B 4G3
or call 1-800-661-9800. Visit our Web site—www.family.org—
to learn more about Focus on the Family or to find out if
there is an associate office in your country.

We'd love to hear from you!

Saving Your Marriage Before It Starts

Seven Questions to Ask Before (and After) You Marry

Drs. Les & Leslie Parrott

Saving Your Marriage Before It Starts is the first comprehensive marriage preparation program specifically designed for today's couples. And it's the first program for couples developed by a couple, Les and Leslie Parrott.

Having tasted firsthand the difficulties of "wedding bell blues," they show young couples the skills they need to make the transition from "single" to "married" smooth and enjoyable. Whether you're contemplating marriage, engaged, or newly married, Les and Leslie will lead you through the thorniest spot in establishing a relationship. You'll learn how to uncover and deal with problems before they emerge. You'll discover how to communicate, not just talk. And you'll learn the importance of becoming "soul mates"—a couple committed to growing together spiritually.

Saving Your Marriage Before It Starts is more than a book—it's practically a premarital counseling session! Questions at the end of every chapter help you explore each topic personally. Companion men's and women's workbooks full of self-tests and exercises will help you apply what you learn. And the *Saving Your Marriage Before It Starts* video curriculum will help you learn and grow with other couples who are dealing with the same struggles and questions. So start today, while your love is fresh. Save your marriage—before it starts.

Hardcover: 0-310-49240-8
Leader's Guide: 0-310-20448-8
Workbook for Men: 0-310-48731-5
Workbook for Women: 0-310-48741-2
Curriculum Kit: 0-310-20451-8

Pick up a copy at your favorite bookstore!

ZONDERVAN™

GRAND RAPIDS, MICHIGAN 49530 USA

Saving Your Second Marriage Before It Starts

*Nine Questions to Ask Before
(and After) You Remarry*

Drs. Les & Leslie Parrott

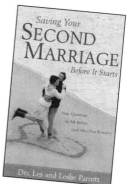

Sixty percent of second marriages fail. Yours can be among the ones that succeed. Relationship experts Les and Leslie Parrott show how you can beat the odds with flying colors and make remarriage the best thing that's ever happened to you. Do you have the skills you need? Now is the time to acquire them—and build a future together that is everything marriage can and ought to be.

Hardcover: 0-310-20748-7
Workbook for Men: 0-310-24054-9
Workbook for Women: 0-310-24055-7
Abridged Audio Pages® Cassette: 0-310-24066-2

Pick up a copy at your favorite bookstore!

GRAND RAPIDS, MICHIGAN 49530 USA

When Bad Things Happen to Good Marriages

How to Stay Together When Life Pulls You Apart

Drs. Les & Leslie Parrott

No matter how good your marriage is, it's not invulnerable. Bad things happen to the best of marriages. The question isn't whether you'll face struggles as a couple, but how you'll handle them when they come. When the going gets tough, what does it take to preserve—and in the long run, even strengthen—your union?

Relationship experts and award-winning authors Les and Leslie Parrott believe the same forces that can destroy a marriage can become the catalyst for new relational depth and richness—provided you make wise choices. You can even survive any of the four most heartbreaking crises a marriage can endure: infidelity, addiction, infertility, and loss. The stories and insights of couples who have made it through the worst will encourage you that your marriage is worth fighting for, not just because quitting is so devastating but because the rewards of sticking it out are so great.

The Parrotts explain why every marriage starts out good but inevitably bumps into bad things. Designed for use with its accompanying, individual workbooks for husbands and wives, *When Bad Things Happen to Good Marriages* could be a lifesaver for your relationship. It can make the difference between a marriage that founders on the shoals of circumstance and one that grows through hardship to release undreamed-of goodness and blessing in your lives.

Hardcover: 0-310-22459-4
Workbook for Husbands: 0-310-23902-8
Workbook for Wives: 0-310-23903-6
Abridged Audio Pages® Cassette: 0-310-22977-4

Pick up a copy at your favorite bookstore!

ZONDERVAN™

GRAND RAPIDS, MICHIGAN 49530 USA